CHRISTIAN HEROES: THEN & NOW

SUNDAR SINGH

Footprints Over the Mountains

Christian Heroes: Then & Now

Sundar Singh

Footprints Over the Mountains

Janet & Geoff Benge

YWAM Publishing is the publishing ministry of Youth With A Mission (YWAM), an international missionary organization of Christians from many denominations dedicated to presenting Jesus Christ to this generation. To this end, YWAM has focused its efforts in three main areas: (1) training and equipping believers for their part in fulfilling the Great Commission (Matthew 28:19), (2) personal evangelism, and (3) mercy ministry (medical and relief work).

For a free catalog of books and materials, call (425) 771-1153 or (800) 922-2143.
Visit us online at www.ywampublishing.com.

Sundar Singh: Footprints Over the Mountains

Published by YWAM Publishing
a ministry of Youth With A Mission
P.O. Box 55787, Seattle, WA 98155

Library of Congress Cataloging-in-Publication Data
Benge, Janet, 1958–
Sundar Singh : footprints over the mountains / Janet and Geoff Benge.
p. cm. — (Christian heroes, then & now)
Includes bibliographical references.
ISBN 1-57658-318-X
1. Singh, Sundar, 1889—Juvenile literature. 2. Mystics—India—Biography— Juvenile literature. I. Benge, Geoff, 1954– II. Title. III. Series.
BV5095.S5B46 2005
266′.0092—dc22 2004030061

ISBN 978-1-57658-318-0 (paperback)
ISBN 978-1-57658-603-7 (e-book)

Scripture quotations are taken from the King James Version of the Bible.

Fourth printing 2017

Printed in the United States of America

Christian Heroes: Then & Now

Adoniram Judson
Amy Carmichael
Betty Greene
Brother Andrew
Cameron Townsend
Charles Mulli
Clarence Jones
Corrie ten Boom
Count Zinzendorf
C. S. Lewis
C. T. Studd
David Bussau
David Livingstone
Dietrich Bonhoeffer
D. L. Moody
Elisabeth Elliot
Eric Liddell
Florence Young
Francis Asbury
George Müller
Gladys Aylward
Hudson Taylor
Ida Scudder
Isobel Kuhn
Jacob DeShazer
Jim Elliot
John Flynn
John Wesley
John Williams
Jonathan Goforth
Klaus-Dieter John
Lillian Trasher
Loren Cunningham
Lottie Moon
Mary Slessor
Mildred Cable
Nate Saint
Paul Brand
Rachel Saint
Richard Wurmbrand
Rowland Bingham
Samuel Zwemer
Sundar Singh
Wilfred Grenfell
William Booth
William Carey

Available in paperback, e-book, and audiobook formats.Unit study curriculum guides are available for select biographies.

www.HeroesThenAndNow.com

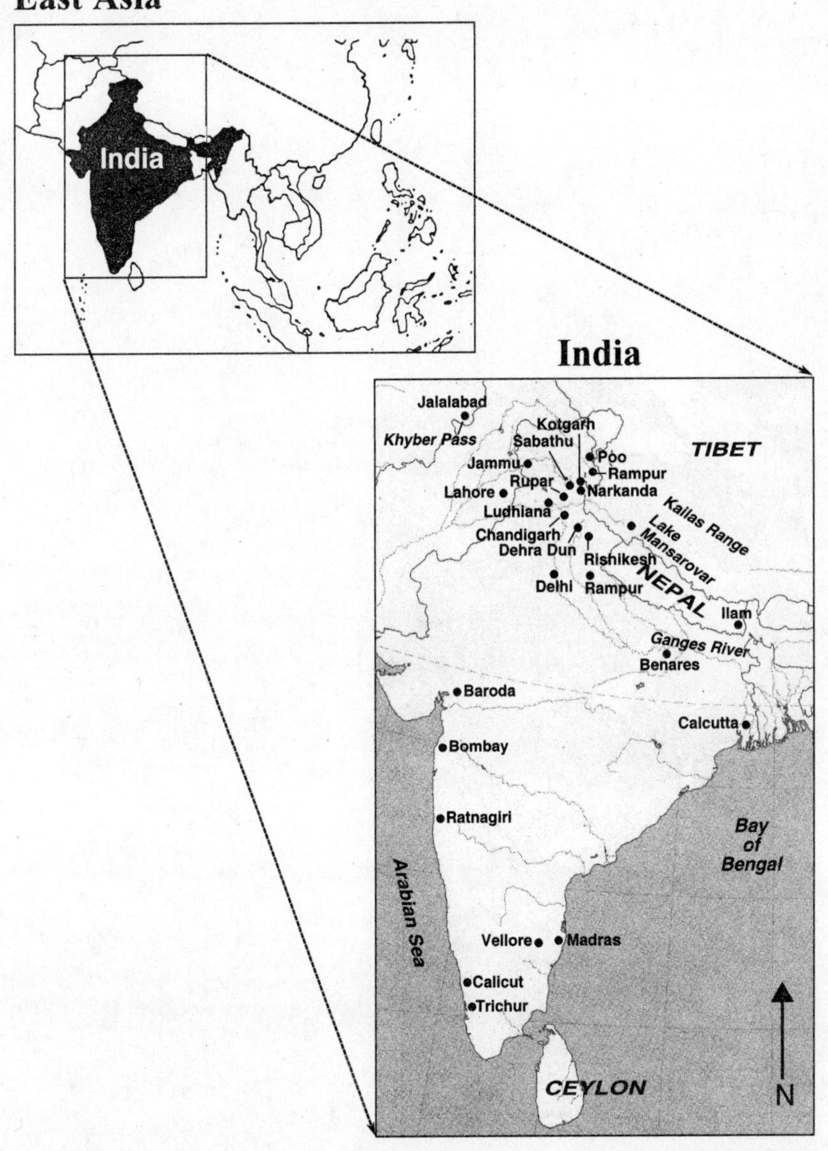
East Asia
India
India
Jalalabad
Khyber Pass
Kotgarh
Sabathu
TIBET
Poo
Jammu
Rampur
Rupar
Narkanda
Lahore
Ludhiana
Kailas Range
Chandigarh
Lake Mansarovar
Dehra Dun
Rishikesh
NEPAL
Delhi
Rampur
Ilam
Ganges River
Benares
Baroda
Calcutta
Bombay
Ratnagiri
Bay of Bengal
Arabian Sea
Vellore
Madras
Calicut
Trichur
CEYLON
N

Contents

Chapter 1

He Had Saved His Own Life

Sundar Singh gasped a breath of icy, thin air at the summit of the pass. His head was spinning from the sixteen-thousand-foot altitude, his lungs throbbed, and his bare feet had gone completely numb hours before. Another traveler, a Tibetan he had met the day before, trudged along beside Sundar, who was glad for the man's company. After several minutes of rest, the two men began their descent from the heights of the Himalayan Mountains. They hoped to reach a small village perched precariously on the edge of a steep precipice at the bottom of the trail before darkness engulfed them.

The two men were halfway down the trail when the wind whipped up and the air became bitterly cold. Sundar began to fear that they might not make it to the village, which was still several miles away, especially since the trail had narrowed to a foot-wide, slippery ledge and their going was slow. On previous trips across these mountains, he had come upon the bodies of men frozen to death by such sudden change in the weather, and he hoped and prayed that the same fate did not await him.

Sundar tried not to look down as he clawed his way along the narrow ledge, but as his eyes scanned the rock ahead for his next foothold, something far below caught his attention: a brown object lying on the snow. As Sundar studied the object, he realized that it was the body of a man. Then, surprisingly, one of the body's arms flailed—the man was alive!

Sundar tugged at the fur jacket of his traveling companion. "Look down," he yelled into the howling wind. "A man has fallen down there. We must try to rescue him."

Sundar's traveling companion shook his head vigorously. "If we try to rescue that man, none of us will reach the village," he yelled back. "We will all freeze. We must get to the village. That man is already as good as dead. Leave him to his fate."

"I can't," Sundar replied. "Please help me to go down and get him. It will take both of us."

The traveling companion shook his head again. "If you value your life, you will come with me." Without even looking back, he turned and continued picking his way along the ledge.

Sundar looked around for a way down to the man. When he thought he had found one, he climbed off the edge of the ledge and hand over hand made his way down the rock face. He willed his numb toes to grip the crevices in the rock. It was treacherous going, and Sundar prayed the entire way, but finally he made it to the bottom of the ravine where the fallen traveler lay.

Kneeling down beside the man, Sundar took a closer look at him. The man's hair and beard were frozen, and he was barely breathing, but none of his bones appeared to be broken.

"Come on, let's get you out of here," Sundar said, standing up and heaving the man onto his back. He pulled his blanket around them both and tied it in front, forming a cradle for the man. Then slowly and painstakingly Sundar inched his way back up the side of the ravine. The extra weight of the man on his back caused Sundar's numb feet to bleed and throb as they beat against the jagged ice and razor-sharp rock, but eventually Sundar reached the safety of the ledge and began carrying the man along the trail.

Soon Sundar was leaving bloodred stains in the snow with each step, as slowly but surely he inched his way forward. He dared not to stop, even when it began to snow heavily, reducing visibility and making the trail even more slippery. Stopping meant certain death for both of them.

As the daylight began to fade, Sundar wondered whether they would make it to the village before nightfall, when it would be impossible to make out the trail in the darkness. Thankfully, right then the snow let up, and in the improved visibility Sundar could make out a cluster of stone houses a few hundred yards ahead. Relief overcame him, until he took a few more steps. There at the side of the trail lay the frozen body of his traveling companion. The man's eyes were open, and his hands were frozen to his face.

Since he could do nothing for the man, given the conditions, Sundar trudged on. Soon he and the man he was carrying on his back were safely inside one of the small, round huts, sitting in front of a yak-dung fire. As Sundar sat sipping a cup of hot tea, he realized that he also could well have frozen to death. What had saved him from such a fate was the man he was carrying on his back. The contact of their two bodies had produced enough heat to stave off the savage cold and keep both men warm. In risking his life to rescue the fallen traveler, Sundar had unwittingly saved his own life.

As he drifted off to sleep in front of the fire, Sundar imagined some of the trials that lay ahead of him in Tibet. This day's ordeal would not be the last life-threatening event on his mission trip; he was sure of that. But he was sure of something else as well: ever since he had been a small boy growing up in the Sikh village of Rampur on the Punjab plain of northern India, God's hand had been upon him.

Chapter 2

The Path That Will Lead You to God

Sundar Singh squinted against the bright sunlight as he followed his mother across the dusty Punjab plain. Despite the grit in his eyes and the sun beating down on his turban-covered head, Sundar felt like bursting into song. Today, September 3, 1896, was his seventh birthday. Even better than that, it was the day his mother declared him ready to recite the Bhagavad Gita to the holy man, whom they had visited together for as long as Sundar could remember.

As he walked, Sundar thought of his older brothers, who had laughed at him as he and his mother left the house in Rampur village to visit the holy man. "Ha," they had said. "Too much religion will make a little head like yours pop! How are all those words going to help you become a banker or a lawyer?"

His mother had raised her hand to them. "Stop now," she said. "Every one of you has his own path to walk, and Sundar has his, too. Only God can tell what he is preparing Sundar for."

As Sundar thought of his mother's words, he loved her even more for saying them. She was known as one of the holiest women in the region, a *bhakta,* or saint, some people called her. Although Sundar's father, Sher Singh, was not particularly interested in religious matters, Sundar knew that he, too, was proud of his mother and her gentle ways. Although the family was Sikh, his mother often said, "God speaks in many ways and through many faiths." As a result, she encouraged Sundar to understand the good in all religions.

That is why on this particularly hot September afternoon Sundar and his mother were on their way to visit the holy man, or *sadhu,* as holy men were called, to recite to him not the Sikh scriptures but Hindu scripture.

Most seven-year-old boys living in India in 1896 had not yet learned much about their faith, but Sundar was an exception. He spent hours listening to various religious teachers in the Sikh temples. In addition to memorizing the entire Bhagavad Gita, he knew large tracts of the Sikh scriptures, the Granth Sahib. He also knew that Guru Nanak had started the Sikh religion in 1496. The guru had been born into a simple Hindu family and worked among Muslims, and by the time he was twenty-seven years old, he had started a religion. He worshiped one eternal God and rejected the Hindu caste system, insisting instead that, in God's eyes, men and women, rich and poor, were all alike. Now, four hundred years later, the Sikh religion was thriving in North India. And its followers still believed that there was one benevolent God.

Sundar and his mother followed a winding path that led them to the edge of a forest. There, sitting in the shade of a tree, was the sadhu, clad in a yellow robe. The sadhu welcomed the two of them warmly and then proceeded to ask Sundar some questions. As Sundar answered, the sadhu's eyes lit up, and finally he said, "Now you must recite the Bhagavad Gita for me."

The holy man sat cross-legged on the ground, his back straight as he waited for Sundar to begin. Sundar cleared his throat and began to recite the Hindu text in Sanskrit. At first he was nervous, and the words tumbled from his mouth in a halting, high-pitched voice. But as his nervousness subsided, his words started to flow with confidence.

Sundar got so caught up in the recitation that he was not sure how long he had been speaking when the holy man finally raised his hand. "You may stop now. You have done well," he said.

With that, Sundar stood tall and thrust out his chest.

Then the sadhu spoke again. "You have recited well, yes, but you are proud at having done so. Pride is the enemy. You must learn humility as well as the Bhagavad Gita. Humility is the path that will lead you to God."

Sundar knew that the holy man was right. Pride was exactly what he was feeling. He was proud at having recited the Bhagavad Gita so well. As he thought about the sadhu's words, his shoulders slumped, and he diverted his eyes to the dusty ground.

"What does the Bhagavad Gita say is the way to please God?" the sadhu asked.

"It tells us that the way to pleasing God is by keeping all the laws that have been handed down to us by our forefathers."

"And?" the sadhu questioned further.

"It also tells us that to please God we must practice the way of meditation and self-denial. That we must cut ourselves off from the ideas of men and think only on the things of God," Sundar said.

"You have spoken correctly," the holy man said with a look of satisfaction. Then he added, "If you do these things, the day may come when you, too, can call yourself a sadhu. Now it is time for you to go. But do not forget what we have spoken of."

"I will not," Sundar replied as he and his mother turned and set out for home.

That night, and for many nights afterward, Sundar thought about what the sadhu had told him. He wondered about how he might become holy. He read the Sikh scriptures for hours at a time, until his father complained that so much reading and religious thinking was bad for his health. Despite his father's objections, Sundar could feel something tugging at his heart—he wanted to find the way to God. He determined that part of finding his way to God would be to do good whenever the opportunity arose.

One day not too long afterward, Sundar's father gave him a rupee to spend on whatever he liked at the local bazaar. Sundar took the money and ran off, trying to decide which of his favorite sweets he would buy. At the edge of the bazaar Sundar saw a beggar woman. She was skin and bone, her hair was matted, her dark eyes were glazed over and sunken, and she was shivering uncontrollably. Sundar had seen her before but had never stopped to really look at her. Suddenly he remembered his decision to do good wherever he could. Here was a woman who desperately needed help, and he could help her. He slipped his hand into his pocket and pulled out the rupee his father had given him. He could do without the sweets.

"Here, take this," Sundar said, handing the woman the rupee.

Tears formed at the edges of the woman's sunken eyes as she reached out and took the coin and thanked Sundar for it.

A warm feeling of satisfaction swept through Sundar at his kind deed. But was there more he could do? Yes, there was. Sundar turned and ran back to the family compound.

"Father, Father," he called as he ran in the gate.

Sundar found his father inside sitting at a table making entries in a ledger.

"Father, I need ten rupees," he began breathlessly. "There is a beggar woman at the bazaar. She is very sick and needs our help. I gave her my rupee, but it is not nearly enough. With ten rupees she can buy food and a blanket to keep warm."

Sher Singh put down his pen and looked directly at his son. "Sundar, I cannot give you ten rupees. First, it is a lot of money. But if I give you the money to give to this woman, every sick beggar in Rampur and the surrounding area will be coming to our gate expecting the same treatment. No, that will not do. I will not give you the money. You have done what you can; now let someone else take care of her."

"But—" Sundar began.

His father raised his hand to stop him. "Enough, Sundar. I have spoken."

As his father picked up the pen and again began making entries in the ledger, Sundar turned and left the room. And that was when he saw it. Right there on the sideboard in the living room was his father's money pouch. At first Sundar tried not to think about it, but an idea formed in his head and would not let go. No, he told himself, he could not steal money from his father's money pouch. But then a picture of the beggar woman flashed through his mind. She needed his help. Before he knew it, Sundar had picked up the money pouch and slid a ten-rupee note from it. *Father will never notice that it is missing,* he reassured himself.

Sundar ran all the way back to the bazaar. He was out of breath when he spotted the frail form of the beggar woman. He stopped short, thinking about what he was about to do. Suddenly he was confused. How could he steal from his father? Surely that one wrong would undo all the good he was trying to do for the beggar woman. If he followed through with this action, he might find himself farther away from God, not closer to Him. Despite desperately wanting to help the beggar woman some more, Sundar turned around and began winding his way through the streets toward home. Less than half an hour had passed since he had taken the money, too little time, he reasoned, for anyone to notice that the money was gone. He would just slip the ten-rupee note back into his father's money pouch, and no one would ever know what he had done.

Sundar was surprised when he walked through the gate into the family compound. His father was storming back and forth in the yard. "Ah, there you are. Some money is missing from my pouch, ten rupees to be exact. Do you know anything about it, Sundar?"

Sundar wanted to say yes and hand over the banknote, but he could not. He could see the anger in his father's eyes, and he feared the punishment that would be meted out to him. Then Sundar heard himself say, "No, I know nothing of the missing money."

"Then it must be one of the servants," Sundar's father said in a determined voice. "I will get to the bottom of this. We cannot tolerate a thief in the house."

Hardly able to comprehend the situation he had gotten himself into, Sundar turned and left the compound. This time he went to the woods on the outskirts of the village to think and be alone. What a mess he had made of things. All he wanted to do was help the beggar woman at the bazaar, but now he was nothing but a liar and a thief.

The sun was beginning to set when Sundar finally began making his way home. When he arrived, he learned that his father had had the house servants beaten as punishment for stealing money from him. Sundar's mother explained that since none of the servants would own up to the crime, Sher Singh was left with no other option but to punish them all. Sundar was horrified at where his actions had led.

That night Sundar could neither eat nor sleep. As he tossed and turned on his sleeping mat, his conscience gnawed at him. How could he ever look his father in the eye again? Or the servants, knowing that they had endured the punishment that should have been his? Finally Sundar could stand it no longer. Even though it was midnight, he had to set the matter straight. He stumbled to his feet and went to wake his father.

Sundar trembled as he shook his father awake. Sher Singh looked surprised and then shocked as Sundar handed him the ten-rupee note and confessed what he had done.

When he had finished his confession, Sundar stood tensely, waiting for the beating he knew would follow. But to his surprise, instead of telling Sundar to get the whip, his father reached up and put his arm around him. "Sundar, I have always trusted you. And your confession convinces me that I was not wrong in that trust. Now run along to bed, and we will talk more in the morning."

The following morning when Sundar awoke, his father was waiting for him, his money pouch in hand. Sher Singh pulled the ten-rupee note from it and handed it to Sundar. "Take this and buy the beggar woman some food and a blanket," he said. And then he pulled out a one-rupee coin. "And here, take this and buy yourself some sweets while you are at the bazaar."

"Thank you, Father, thank you," Sundar said, taking the money, scarcely able to comprehend his father's kindness. He quickly dressed and headed for the bazaar.

Soon after this incident, Sundar began attending the American Presbyterian mission school near his home. Most of the other boys in Rampur were forbidden from attending a Christian school, and they would not have wanted to anyway. Sikhs were taught to despise Christians because Christians believed that God had come down and taken on the form of a man. But Sundar's mother was different. She had made friends with two of the foreign female missionaries and decided to enroll her youngest son in their school.

Sundar was happy to attend the school. Indeed he enjoyed it greatly, until he was fourteen and a terrible thing happened—his mother died. Sundar was devastated. All of his religious acts—his praying, visiting the temple and the sadhu, reciting the Bhagavad Gita, even learning about God from the Christian Bible—had been encouraged by his mother. And now, unexplainably, she was gone.

Sundar's mother had also taught him about the Hindu belief in reincarnation, how each soul is destined to pass through an almost endless cycle of death and rebirth until finally it attains the merit needed to once and for all pass from this world. Sundar had accepted his mother's words, but now he found no comfort whatsoever in reincarnation. The thought that her soul might be reborn as someone else whom he would not recognize saddened and distressed him.

The missionaries tried to comfort Sundar with words from the Bible, but he spat their words back in their faces. He thought bitterly about the fool he had been for hoping in God and trying to find and serve Him. His heart grew hard, and within a month of his mother's dying, he was impossible for the Christian teachers to control. He argued with them at every turn, using his quick mind to refute anything they said in Bible study. He quoted long passages from the Hindu, Sikh, and Buddhist scriptures to back up his points.

Finally Sundar announced to his father that he would not be going back to the mission school.

He would rather walk three miles each way to the public school. His father let him go, and Sundar did everything he could to purge the Christian teaching from his mind. On his own, he found this more difficult to do than he had anticipated, so he gathered together a group of young hooligans to harass the Christians in the village. Sundar's hatred for Christians grew, and he vowed not to rest until the Christians were driven from the village. Sundar's father tried to reason with his son, but Sundar would not listen. Now that his mother was dead, he did not care what anyone thought of him.

Finally summer arrived, and with it the relentless heat of the plains. Sundar soon found it more and more difficult to walk the six miles to school and back. He realized why one morning, when he could not get up from his sleeping mat. Despite the summer heat, his entire body shook, and he felt very cold. He had caught malaria.

Chapter 3

The Biggest Shock of His Life

The malaria Sundar had contracted wracked his body for most of the summer, leaving him feeling listless and depressed. As fall approached, when school would start again, Sundar could not imagine walking six miles a day to school and back. Reluctantly he allowed his father to make inquiries about reenrolling at the nearby mission school.

Despite Sundar's previous disruptive behavior, the school principal, the Reverend Newton, agreed to have him back. And so Sundar returned to his old school. He no longer heckled his teachers or threw stones at them, but he did not learn much from them either. After suffering through malaria, Sundar now found that his mind wandered easily, and he often slept between classes. He became convinced that the lingering effects of the malaria would kill him before he ever graduated from school, and that prospect made him gloomier than ever.

His gloom quickly turned to anger, which he did not direct at his teachers this time but at the Christian God. Finally, one day after Bible study, Sundar asked his teacher to sell him a copy of the New Testament. The teacher readily agreed, and his smile told Sundar that he was hoping for a change in attitude as Sundar read the book. But Sundar had no intention of reading the New Testament. He had other plans for it.

That evening Sundar called his friends together in the yard of the Singh house. He disappeared into the kitchen and emerged a few minutes later with a bundle of sticks and a can of kerosene. He piled the sticks on the ground and then doused them with kerosene. When he was satisfied that the sticks had soaked up enough of the accelerant, Sundar laid the tin aside and struck a match. He dropped it onto the sticks, and with a *whoosh* they leapt into flames. The glow of the fire filled the yard and danced on the faces of the boys standing around it. When Sundar was sure he had everyone's attention, he stepped forward and dramatically held up the New Testament. Without saying a word he opened the book and began tearing the pages from it one by one. He dropped them into the fire and watched as they burst into flame.

At first Sundar felt elated, but as the flames curled around the edges of the last pages of the

New Testament, he felt a surge of remorse pulse through him. He could picture his mother's face. He wondered what she would think of his burning the Christian scriptures. She had taught him that every religion had value. Sundar reminded himself that he doubted this was true. Besides, the Christian God had not struck him dead for burning the New Testament. Obviously the Christian God was not a live God. He was just a collection of lies gathered in a book. But then another thought hit Sundar. What about the Hindu gods and the Sikh gurus? Were they true, or were they just lies as well?

Suddenly Sundar was gripped with the need to know for certain. He was still sick and depressed from the malaria, and he felt he could no longer take his mother's word on anything. After all, God, whoever or whatever He might be, had taken his mother from him. And unlike his older brothers, Sundar did not think life was worth living unless he had answers to the God question once and for all. As he thought about this, he heard the whistle of a train in the distance as it passed close by Rampur, and it gave Sundar an idea.

It was a strange idea, but it would not go away. On the third night after burning the New Testament, Sundar lay awake thinking about it. Finally he decided he had to act. He climbed off his sleeping mat, pulled his robe around him, and silently made his way to the bathing room at the back of the house. Mechanically he drew water from the well and poured it over himself. He shivered with cold, but that was the point. Tonight was the night he would know for sure whether there was a God. There was an inevitability about his actions as he put his robe back on and retreated to his room. Sundar sat on his sleeping mat and prayed. "God, if You are there, reveal Yourself to me tonight. If You do not, I will kill myself in the morning, because I cannot live another day with all of these unanswered questions." Then he sat and waited.

Sundar's decision to kill himself was not an idle threat. At five o'clock every morning the train to Lahore rolled past Rampur. If he had not received an answer from God by then, Sundar was determined to lie on the railway tracks and wait for the train to roll over him. He had decided that it would be better to be dead than to continue his meaningless life.

One hour passed, and then two. Sundar was still wide awake and listening for any sound, any sign that God might be there. Four thirty rolled by, and Sundar's mind began to think about the train and what he would have to do. He had decided the easiest and quickest way to end his life was to rest his head right on the rail and let the train crush it. But right in the middle of this morbid thought Sundar became aware of a glow in the room. At first he thought it was something outside shining through the bedroom window. But the shutter on the window was closed. The glow grew brighter and brighter until it became a piercing white light. Then the figure of a man appeared at the center of the light.

Whether the figure was actually in his bedroom or just in his imagination, Sundar could not tell. All he knew was that what he was seeing was real to him. He strained to see the figure in the light, and that is when he received the biggest shock of his life. He had expected it to be Krishna or perhaps Buddha, but it was neither. Instead he recognized the figure as Jesus Christ. But how could it be? Sundar was convinced that Jesus Christ was long dead. Yet here He was, His piercing eyes burrowing into Sundar's heart.

Then the figure spoke to him in perfect Hindustani. "How long will you persecute Me? I have come to save you. You were praying to know the right way. Why do you not take it? I am the Way."

At these words Sundar clambered onto his knees and began to pray. Fervently he asked Jesus Christ to forgive him and change him.

The vision finally faded, and as Sundar got up from his knees, he heard the whistle of the train in the distance. But all thoughts of taking his life were now gone. Instead Sundar felt an incredible sense of peace and joy flood over him. He *had* to tell someone about what had happened. Amazingly, the Jesus the missionaries talked about was alive, and He was the true Son of God!

Sundar ran into his father's bedroom. "Father, wake up! I have something to tell you," he said, shaking his father awake.

Sher Singh opened his bleary eyes. "What is it?"

"Father, it is wonderful news. I have seen Him, Jesus Christ. He came to me in my room, and He spoke to me in Hindustani."

Sundar's father sat up and wiped the sleep from his eyes. "What are you talking about, son?" he asked. "Three days ago you burned the Christian book, and now you are telling me you believe what it says? Are you touched in the head?"

Sundar stared at his father, desperate to think of a way to make him understand. But before he could do so, Sher Singh put his hand on his son's shoulder. "Go back to bed now, and in the morning you will realize how foolish you are being. It is just a dream, and you must not make yourself over-excited with such imaginings," he said.

Sundar made his way back to his bedroom and lay down, but he could not sleep. How amazing it was to think that Jesus was alive. No wonder the missionaries came from halfway across the world to tell the people of India about their God. Sundar was sure that he would do the same now that he knew that everything the Christians had told him about God was true.

When breakfast was served later that morning, Sundar's father busied himself talking to his older sons. Sundar's heart dropped as he realized that his father was not going to bring up the subject of what had happened during the night. Sundar knew that he would have to do it himself.

"Father," he began. "About last night..."

Sher Singh waved his hand to stop Sundar. "Do not worry about it, son. It was the product of reading Christian books at school. They have played tricks on your mind at night. I will not mention it again, and neither should you."

"But, Father," Sundar said, desperation rising in his voice, "it was all true! I did see Jesus in the night, and I had just bathed in cold water, so I am sure I was not asleep. Besides, I feel different this morning."

Two of Sundar's older brothers snickered.

"I do feel different," he went on, "and I am not ashamed to say it. I am a Christian now, and I will be until the day I die."

Sundar's father's voice was serious and low as he said, "Now that would be very foolish, son. You are a Sikh, Sundar, not a Christian. You are the son of the son of a Sikh, your brothers are Sikhs, you will marry a Sikh and raise your children to be Sikh. It is a proud and strong heritage. Do you understand me?"

Sundar nodded. Of course he understood. He had always expected these things for himself, until now. But the vision of Jesus Christ had changed everything, and he knew he had to be true to that vision.

"Father, I will do anything in the world to please you, except for this," Sundar said respectfully. "I have been searching for God, and now I have found Him. I will not let Him go, even if my life depends on it."

"It well might," Sundar heard his oldest brother mumble under his breath.

Chapter 4

"We Reject You Forever"

"There he goes!" one of Sundar's old friends yelled as Sundar rounded a corner on his way to the market. "Get him!"

Suddenly Sundar found his way blocked by the same group of hooligans he had led over the summer.

"Tell us you're not a Christian," one of them yelled. "It's impossible."

"Yes, we want to hear it from your own lips. Have you turned your back on Sikhs to follow the Englishman's God?" another asked.

Sundar felt his heart beating under his muslin shirt. He took a deep breath and faced his friends. "It is true," he said. "I did not wish to become a Christian, but Jesus appeared to me, and now I want to serve Him for the rest of my life."

"It could be a short life," laughed the tallest boy in the group as he produced a stout stick from behind his back. "What do you say now? Are you so sure that's what you want?"

Sundar nodded. "Whether I live or die does not matter. I belong to Jesus Christ, and that is enough for me," he said.

A nervous twitter of laughter arose from the group, and then the boys turned and walked away.

"We'll get you later," one of the boys shouted over his shoulder.

The mangoes and rice that Sundar had been sent to buy no longer seemed important. He walked past the market and found himself on the road that led to the holy man. He knew it well. It was the same road he had walked at least a hundred times with his mother. How he missed her. Now he wished she were still alive. He was positive she would have understood his quest and not mocked his new faith. She would have talked to Sher Singh on his behalf. But she was gone, and now there was no one to speak up for him. Sundar knew that his father was angry and embarrassed that he had converted to Christianity. Being a Sikh involved more than just religious beliefs. All Sikhs considered one another brothers, and to seal that bond, they all took the last name Singh. Singh, as Sundar had learned at his father's knee, meant lion, and Sikhs were strong and brave—and true to one another. And now Sundar had broken that bond, betraying every Singh in India. It was a heavy burden to bear, and he could only pray that God would show him the way to get through the terrible crisis.

Eventually Sundar turned around and began walking back to Rampur, sure of only one thing—he had taken the name of Christ, and if that meant losing everything else, it was a trade-off he was prepared to make.

Thankfully, things went better at school. The Christian teachers prayed with Sundar and encouraged him not to give up his new faith. They told him that he was a natural leader and that if he stood up for Christ, other boys would follow his lead. And they did. Within a month three other Sikh boys were converted, and Sundar and the three others asked to be baptized. That was when trouble really began in Rampur. The people of the village could accept one convert, especially since Sundar had always been somewhat of a religious young man, but four boys snubbing the faith of their fathers was too much.

Sundar's enthusiasm for his new faith had unknowingly inflamed the attitudes of the people of Rampur toward the missionaries, and the situation became dangerous. The Reverend Newton, principal of the Christian school, was brought before a magistrate and ordered to account for polluting the boys' faith. The magistrate ordered the school to be shut down, and two of the new converts buckled under the pressure and renounced their Christian faith and returned to Sikhism. The third boy, Gurdit Singh, fled to a mission station two hundred miles away at Khanna, where reports coming back to Rampur said he had been baptized.

Sundar watched in shock as these events unfolded around him. Before he became a Christian, he had vowed to bring down the Christian school. Now, ironically, his conversion had played a large part in seeing the school closed. All he could do was pray that the situation would improve.

But it did not. Sundar learned that Gurdit's father had gone to Khanna and pleaded for Gurdit to come home, telling him that his mother was very ill. When Gurdit arrived home, he found that it was a trick to get him back. His mother was in perfect health. Despite the trick, his family appeared to welcome him home and even to tolerate his new religion. But Sundar learned that a week after Gurdit had come home, he was killed. His brothers had poisoned him for disgracing the family name. Things in Sundar's home were fast deteriorating as well. Sundar asked the Reverend Newton for help. The Reverend Newton had decided to stay on in Rampur, even though the school was closed, but he suggested that Sundar enroll in a boarding school for Christian boys at Ludhiana. Sundar thought that this sounded like a good idea, and the Reverend Newton arranged a scholarship for him to cover his fees and bought a train ticket for him to Ludhiana.

Sundar breathed a huge sigh of relief as he walked through the gates of Christian High School. The past few months had been the most difficult of his life, and he was glad to be among people who believed as he did. Sundar soon discovered, however, that most of his fellow students, even the Christian ones, did not share the joy of knowing Jesus Christ that he experienced. Despite all of the Bible study and prayer they engaged in, they seemed to care little about Christianity. Their attitude shocked Sundar, who began to wonder whether he would ever be surrounded by people who thought as he did.

Sundar was despairing over the state of things at the boarding school, when he received a letter from his father. With shaking hands he opened it and read:

> My dear son, the light of my eyes, the comfort of my heart—may you live long. We are all well here and hope the same for you.... I order you to get married immediately!... Make haste and don't disappoint us.... Does the Christian religion teach disobedience to parents?
>
> You have gone mad! Just think for a moment who will take care of all our property! Do you want to blot out the family name? If you get engaged, I will bequeath to you all the sum of money now in the three banks (the interest of which amounts to three or four hundred rupees a month); otherwise you will lose what I have reserved for you.... It will be for your good if you come home at once.... I am not well.

The letter threw Sundar into a quandary. Yes, he had to agree, the Christian religion did teach that children should obey their parents, but it also taught that God must be honored above all else. Sundar did not know what to do.

Over the next few days, he prayed about his future. Should he stay at the boarding school or return home? The memory of Gurdit's fate made thoughts of going home very sobering. However, as Sundar prayed about the situation, he became convinced that he should return to Rampur and live with his family once again.

Sundar was welcomed home by his father and brothers and did his best to fit in once again. But it soon became obvious that his father would not rest until Sundar renounced his Christian faith and returned to his Sikh heritage. On one occasion Sher Singh sent Sundar to visit his rich uncle. The uncle led Sundar into the basement of his house, where he had a large steel vault filled with stacks of banknotes and jewels that sparkled in the light of the oil lamp.

"I will allow you to have all of these riches if you will renounce your new faith and remain in the religion of your fathers and forefathers," he told Sundar.

But Sundar's mind was made up. "Thank you, Uncle," he replied, "but I cannot accept your offer. I must follow the truth as I see it."

With Sundar's refusal of his uncle's offer, persecution began again at home from his father and brothers. So when Sundar's cousin Spuran invited him to come to Nabhu for a visit, Sundar gladly accepted the invitation.

Spuran Singh held high office in the service of the maharaja, or prince, of Nabhu State. The maharaja wielded much power and was revered by all. After Sundar had been in Nabhu two days, the maharaja called him to the palace for an audience.

Sundar was led into the magnificent palace, where the maharaja sat on an ornately carved throne. The maharaja motioned for Sundar to step forward.

"So you are Sundar Singh," he began. "Why do you bring dishonor upon your race? Look, you wear the bracelet of a Sikh, your hair remains uncut in the fashion of the Sikhs, and you bear a Sikh name. So why is it that you do not behave like a Sikh? You are a Singh, the name your ancestors gave to you. Surely you know what it means, don't you?"

Sundar nodded. "Yes, it means lion, my lord," he answered respectfully.

"Then if you bear the name of a lion, why is it that you behave like a jackal?" snapped the maharaja.

Sundar said nothing, and the maharaja continued in a more restrained voice. "Give up this strange religion and return to the faith of your race and of your forefathers. Live up to the name Singh and all it means. If you do this, I am sure a position of honor and power, such as that your cousin Spuran Singh holds, can be found for you here at the palace. Now go and think seriously about what I have said."

"Yes, my lord," Sundar said as he turned and left the palace.

Sundar did think long and hard about what the maharaja had said. And he decided on a course of action. The words the maharaja uttered, "Your hair remains uncut in the fashion of the Sikhs," played over and over in Sundar's mind. When he arrived back in Rampur, Sundar took a pair of scissors and disappeared into his bedroom. Within minutes Sundar had cut off his long locks of jet-black hair.

There was no going back now. Sundar knew that, and that was precisely why he had decided to cut his hair. Every Sikh male was obligated by his religion not to cut his hair—the long hair was curled up tightly in a turban. But under Sundar's turban there was no longer any long hair.

When Sher Singh learned what his son had done, his eyes grew black with rage, and Sundar trembled.

"We reject you forever," his father said.

Sundar knew what was coming next; the words were those of the formal denouncing of a child. They were the most dreaded words a father could say to his son or daughter.

"In the name of the whole family, I declare you are no more worthy to be called our son. We shall have nothing to do with you. We shall forget you as if you had never been born. You will leave this house with nothing but the clothes on your back and never return," his father continued. Then he paused, turned, and pointed to the door, and snapped, "Now go."

Sundar's head was spinning as he opened the door and walked out of his childhood home. At fifteen years of age he was now alone, without family connections or even a place to sleep for the night.

It was twilight, and Sundar wandered in a daze until he came to the edge of the forest, where he made a bed of leaves and lay down. He passed the night fitfully, and in the morning he examined the contents of his pocket. He had his New Testament and enough money to buy a one-way train ticket. But where should he go? Sundar puzzled over the question until finally he decided he should return to Ludhiana and continue his schooling.

The train to Ludhiana was due to pass through Rampur in half an hour. Sundar quickly got up and began making his way to the station. As he walked back into the village, people spat at his feet and cursed him. One woman made a big show of washing herself at the well after Sundar's shadow fell on her. But Sundar hardly noticed the people. He was hungry, and for some reason his stomach was hurting and he was beginning to feel weak.

Sundar had just enough money for the fare to Ludhiana. He took his ticket, climbed onto the train, and found a hard, wooden seat, where he flopped down. How he wished his stomach would stop hurting, but the pain only seemed to get worse. Finally, half an hour into the train trip, Sundar felt the urge to vomit. Quickly he pulled down the window. No sooner had he stuck his head out than the contents of his stomach burst from his mouth. As the vomit ran down the outside of the carriage, Sundar noticed it was mixed with blood. Then the sad realization hit him: his family had poisoned him before they sent him away, and now he was dying.

Sundar was sure that he would not make it alive all the way to Ludhiana, and he prayed that God would show him what to do next. Suddenly he remembered that one of the Christian teachers who had been run out of Rampur when the school was closed had settled in Rupar, the next stop for the train. Sundar decided he would get off the train at Rupar and find the teacher, the Reverend Uppal, and his wife.

It seemed like forever before the train pulled into the station at Rupar. Sundar stumbled from the carriage and made some inquiries as to how to get to the mission house. Somehow he managed to stumble there and knock on the door. The Reverend Uppal opened the door, and Sundar slumped unconscious into his arms.

Sundar was not sure how much time had passed, but when he regained consciousness, he was aware of two men talking outside the room in which he lay on a bed.

"There is nothing more I can do, Mr. Uppal," he heard one of the voices say. "The boy will surely die soon, before the night is over, I expect. There is no point in my giving him any medicine; there is nothing I can give him that will help his condition. I will call again in the morning, and we can make arrangements for his funeral then."

"Yes, thank you very much, Doctor," Sundar heard the Reverend Uppal say.

Die? I am not going to die. God has work He wants me to do. This new resolve swept over Sundar as he lay semiconscious on the bed. And in those moments when he became fully conscious, he prayed fervently that God would heal him.

As the morning sun rose over Rupar, Sundar opened his eyes and began to sit up. His stomach had stopped hurting, and he was beginning to feel his strength return. Mrs. Uppal, who had sat with Sundar throughout the night tending to him, looked shocked. *She looks like she has seen a ghost,* Sundar thought.

"It is all right, Mrs. Uppal," Sundar said in a weak voice. "God has healed me. He has things yet for me to do, and no poison shall stand in the way of His purpose. Now, please help me outside onto the veranda so I can lie in the sun."

Two hours later Sundar was well enough to laugh when the doctor came to visit him. The doctor had come to arrange a funeral, and instead he found his patient sitting outside in the sun well on his way to making a full recovery.

But now that he was feeling better and was not going to die, Sundar had to plan his next step.

Chapter 5

Sadhu Sundar Singh

Now that he had recovered from being poisoned, the obvious choice to Sundar was to continue on to the boarding school at Ludhiana and try to fit in there. And that is what he did, but more problems soon developed. Despite the fact that Sundar's father had declared him dead, when members of his family learned that he had not died from the poison, they followed him to Ludhiana and stormed the gates of the boarding school. They demanded that Sundar return to Rampur with them. The situation was dangerous, and the school principal asked Sundar if for the safety of everyone involved he would be prepared to leave the school.

Sundar agreed, and he was secreted away to the American Presbyterian mission's leprosy hospital at Sabathu, located twenty-three miles from Simla, where Sundar's family had sometimes vacationed when he was a small boy. It had been a tumultuous nine months for Sundar since becoming a Christian, and he was glad to have a place where he could get some rest and peace at last. During the day he helped look after the lepers staying at the hospital, and in the evenings he read the New Testament and prayed about what the future held for him. Some of the American doctors and nurses at Sabathu urged Sundar to go to seminary and train to become a missionary himself, but Sundar was not so sure about the idea. The more time he spent around Indian Christians, the more concerned he became about how they imitated American and English ways of doing things. They wore Western clothes and sang hymns put to English tunes instead of their own Indian melodies. And they seemed to think that it was somehow more Christian to eat Western food and to speak in English.

Sundar looked at Christianity differently. To him the message—the good news that Jesus Christ had come to earth in the form of man and then sacrificed Himself so that humankind could have a relationship with God—had nothing to do with the clothes people wore, the food they ate, or the tunes they sang. He longed to see Indians take Christianity and make it their own, not just an imported religion but something that resonated with their own heritage.

In thinking about this, Sundar was reminded of a scene he had witnessed on a train. At a particular station he watched as a Brahman priest was carried onto the train and placed in a seat near him. Sundar could see that the priest was suffering from heat stroke. The stationmaster must have noticed this too, because he brought the priest a cup of cold water. Sundar watched as the priest refused to drink the water because it came from the unclean cup of a stranger and not from his own brass cup. One of the men who had carried the Brahman onto the train then took the brass cup and poured into it the water that the stationmaster had brought. Then the priest had eagerly taken his brass cup and drunk all of the water.

As Sundar thought about the scene he had witnessed, he realized that Christianity was like the water inside the cup and that it had to be given to the Indian people in a way that they could accept it. Of course he had no idea how he, a fifteen-year-old boy, could make that happen, so he prayed and waited.

Over the next several weeks, Sundar found himself looking northward, toward the snow-covered Himalayas. The majestic mountains glowed pink and gold in the evening sun, and something about them attracted him. The mysterious land of Tibet lay on the other side of the mountains, and although Sundar knew very little about Tibet, he felt that his destiny somehow lay over those high mountains.

On his sixteenth birthday, the day he was legally free from his father's authority, Sundar sought to be baptized in the nearby town of Simla. A Church of England congregation was located there, and the local minister interviewed Sundar and agreed to baptize him. The text chosen for the service was from Psalm 23: "The LORD is my shepherd; I shall not want." There was no going back now. To Sikhs and Hindus, baptism was the absolute point of no return.

Following his baptism, Sundar retreated to the pine forest beyond the hospital. He needed time to think and pray, and he stayed in the forest for a month. At the end of that time he emerged confident of where his future lay. Sundar would become a sadhu, a holy man, like the one his mother had taken him to see so often as a child. The Indian people respected sadhus and would stop to listen to what they had to say. However, unlike the Hindu sadhus Sundar had known, he would tell the story of Jesus and urge the Indian people to seek Him as the bearer of all truth.

This was a bold idea. Sundar did not know of any Christian sadhus. And his idea did not gain the support of many of the English missionaries he knew; the whole concept seemed strange and irrelevant to them. But Sundar was confident that this was the way God was directing him, and so he bought himself the saffron cotton robe and turban that were the hallmarks of a holy man.

On October 6, 1905, sixteen-year-old Sundar, now introducing himself as Sadhu Sundar Singh, set out on foot across the plains of North India. He had no shoes, no money, and few friends, and he was determined never to beg for anything. "I am not worthy to follow in the footsteps of my Lord. But, like Him, I want no home, no possessions. Like Him, I will belong to the road, sharing the sufferings of my people, eating with those who will give me shelter and telling all men of the love of God," he told himself as he set out. "The Lord is my shepherd, and I shall accept whatever He gives me."

Sundar headed toward Simla, stopping in each small village he passed through to share the gospel. Seeing that he wore the saffron robe and turban of a holy man, the people welcomed him into these villages and showed him hospitality and friendship. However, when it became known that Sundar was a Christian and not a Hindu holy man, more often than not he found himself roughly ejected from these villages. As a result he spent many cold, hungry nights sleeping out under the stars. Despite this treatment, Sundar refused to get discouraged. Each morning after a night on the hard ground, he would get up and set off in search of another village in which to share the gospel.

In one village he visited, Sundar spent the day sitting and talking to people about Jesus Christ. Some rejected outright what he said, while others were interested in the things he said. But as night fell, the local people went off to their houses, leaving Sundar alone. Sundar walked over to a tree at the edge of the village and sat down under it. It was then that he realized how hungry he was. He'd had nothing to eat since the few handfuls of rice someone had given him the day before. As he sat under the tree, Sundar began to think about the people of the village in their houses eating rice and vegetables and fruit. How he wished he could be sitting in one of those houses eating. He thought about how good the food would taste and how comfortable he would feel with nourishment in his now empty stomach.

As his mind began to drift off into thoughts of food, Sundar stopped himself. No. These were fruitless thoughts, he told himself. He had chosen to follow God and trust Him to provide for his needs. If He had provided no food for Sundar to eat today, that was fine. Sundar would go to sleep hungry and would not grumble or complain or let his mind run after fanciful thoughts about sitting and eating. Instead he began to sing and praise God. And as he did so, waves of happiness and contentment swept over him.

Sundar had been singing for nearly two hours, when two men from the village walked over to where he was seated. The men looked at him closely, and then one of them looked at the other and said, "He is not drunk; he is happy."

Seeing an opportunity to share the gospel, Sundar explained to the two men why he was singing and that he was happy because he trusted God. The two men listened attentively, and when Sundar had finished speaking, one of the men said, "Please forgive us. It did not occur to us to offer you food. Wait here and we will bring you something to eat."

Several minutes later the two men were back, carrying a basket of food which they offered to Sundar. Sundar took the basket and thanked the men for their generosity, and in no time at all his hunger was satisfied.

As he made his way amid the villages of the Punjab plain, Sundar found himself at a village less than an hour's walk from Rampur. When he had finished in the village, he set out for his hometown. Sundar did not know what kind of reception to expect, and he was pleasantly surprised at the way people welcomed him. Instead of hurling abuse, stones, and rotten fruit and vegetables at him, as they had done in the past, the people invited him into their homes and businesses to talk. They seemed to be genuinely interested when he talked to them about Jesus Christ.

While in Rampur, Sundar sent a message to his father, asking if he could see him. His father's response was swift. He sent a message back saying he did not want to see his son. As far as he was concerned, Sundar was dead.

But Sundar felt he should try again, and so the following day he sent another message to his father, asking to meet him. This time his father relented and invited Sundar to the house for dinner.

Sundar made his way to the Singh family compound and greeted his father. But it was soon obvious to him that his family was not glad to see him and merely tolerated his presence. This was particularly obvious when it came time for dinner. Instead of inviting his son to sit with him and his brothers around the meal, Sher Singh indicated that Sundar should sit separate from the family, explaining that he did not want his son to pollute the food they would eat.

For Sundar it was a bitter blow. He had come, hoping that somehow they could put their differences behind them, but he now realized that was not going to happen. After the family had served themselves, they served Sundar a plate of food, which he ate in silence, sitting cross-legged in the corner of the room.

As Sundar ate, Sher Singh stood and picked up a pitcher of water and walked over to his son. He held the pitcher high and poured the water into Sundar's hands. No matter how he tried, Sundar could not hold back his emotions. Tears welled in his eyes. What his father had just done was a great insult. It was the way Hindus of high caste served the untouchables, the lowest caste members of Indian society. Sher Singh was indicating to his son that he considered him the lowest of the low.

Sundar began to wonder what he had been thinking in hoping for a new start with his family. It was not going to happen. He was as good as dead in their eyes, and he began to wish he could be anywhere but in that room with them. To his relief the meal was soon over, and Sundar stood to leave.

Before he left, Sundar stopped at the door, turned, and said to his father, "It doesn't matter if you have forsaken me. My life now belongs to Christ, and He will not forsake me. His love is unchangeable and greater than your love. Before I became a Christian, I dishonored Jesus Christ, but He did not forsake me. I cannot forsake Him now, and I will not forsake you as you have forsaken me. I thank you for your love to me in the past, and I thank you for allowing me to spend these hours with you under your roof. Good-bye, Father."

With that Sundar turned and walked out of the house. He made his way to the edge of town, where he slept the night under his thin blanket on the hard ground.

The following day Sundar left Rampur, wondering whether he would ever return to the place again. He set out in the direction of the village of Doliwala and arrived there at sunset, just as the storm clouds that had been gathering throughout the day broke and rain began to pour down. Despite the rain, as Sundar walked down the main thoroughfare of the village, people clustered around him, eager for some words from a holy man. But their curiosity soon turned to anger when they realized that Sundar was a Christian sadhu. They picked up rocks and drove him out of their village.

It was dark by now, and Sundar was soaked to the skin. He walked until he came across an abandoned hut by the side of the road. The door was missing, but Sundar was glad for somewhere dry to stay. He was tired from walking all day. He wrapped himself in his thin blanket, found a dry corner, and was soon sound asleep.

As the first shafts of sunlight cut their way through the cracks in the wall of the abandoned hut, Sundar awoke. He reached over to pull up his blanket when something caught his eye. What was it? Was it just a shadow, or was it something else? Sundar peered harder into the early-morning gloom. It was definitely not just a shadow. Rather, it was something long and thick. In an instant Sundar was wide awake. A deadly black cobra was coiled up next to him for warmth! Sundar held his breath as he slid out from under the blanket and edged toward the door. The cobra did not move from its position on the edge of the blanket.

As Sundar reached the doorway of the hut, he thought of the cold winter nights ahead for him. Without his blanket he could freeze to death, but if he woke the sleeping cobra, he could die right there in the hut from one of the snake's poisonous bites. After a brief prayer Sundar decided he needed his blanket and determined to retrieve it. He crept back to where he had been sleeping and gently tugged on the edge of the blanket, never taking his eyes off the snake for a moment. The cobra did not stir as Sundar eased it off his blanket and onto the mud floor. When he finally had the blanket, Sundar headed for the door as silently and as fast as he could. Safely outside the hut, Sundar knelt and thanked God for keeping him safe from the cobra.

Not long after his encounter with the snake, Sundar passed another perilous night. This time he had been in a Muslim village, where he had spent the day preaching in the marketplace without any success. In the evening, as the last rays of the sun disappeared from view, a man cautiously approached Sundar.

"You must leave at once," the man whispered. "There is a plot to kill you. The people think you are a spy."

Sundar nodded and picked up his blanket. He had nowhere to go except out into the barren land outside the village that was infested with dangerous wild animals.

Chapter 6

The Life of a Traveling Sadhu

Sundar found a sheltered, rocky crevice in which to spend the night. But he did not get much sleep. He lay awake most of the night, wrapped in his blanket, listening for the sound of jackals and tigers while swarming insects buzzed around him. And as the temperature dropped, he shivered with cold. He was grateful that no animals bothered him in the darkness, and he was very glad when the first vestiges of dawn crept across the land. He was soon up gathering twigs to build a fire. Sundar was sitting by the fire warming himself and praying about where to go next, when he noticed a group of men approaching. The men were carrying sticks and laughing among themselves. Sundar recognized one of the men—a Muslim man from the village who had hurled stones at him the day before.

Sundar stood and waited, his muscles tightening. He expected the men to mete out a beating to him with their sticks. He was surprised when this did not happen. Instead, when the group of men reached Sundar, their leader fell to his knees. "Please forgive us," he said. "You are a holy man, and we have sinned against you. This morning we agreed to meet at dawn and go beyond the village wall to make sure that wild animals had killed you during the night. But not only are you alive, you are well and waiting for us with peace in your eyes. It is obvious that God especially favors you. Come back to the village with us, and we will give you food and shelter. When you have rested, we will listen to all you have to say."

It took Sundar a moment or two to accept what the man was saying. The man had come to make sure that Sundar was dead, and now he wanted to honor him.

"Only God could turn your hearts," Sundar finally replied. "I will accompany you back to your village and tell you the good news of eternal life."

The men all walked back to the village, and true to their word, they fed and housed Sundar while he preached in the village. Sundar stayed in the village for a week, and when he left, the men asked him to return soon and tell them more of the strange stories of Jesus.

Sundar promised he would return and then set off to the west to find another village in which he could preach the gospel. He had gone only a few miles when he met another sadhu. This sadhu, however, was a Hindu and had discarded his yellow robe and was lying on a bed of nails at the side of the road. Sundar walked over to him and asked, "To what end do you wound and torture yourself so?"

"I see you are a sadhu too. Yet you do not know why I do this? It is my penance. In lying on this bed of nails, I am destroying the flesh and its desires. I serve God in this way, but I am still very aware of my sins and evil heart. Indeed, the weight of my evil heart is more painful than these nails. My goal is to kill all desire and so to find release from myself and oneness with God," the sadhu answered.

"And how long have you been on this quest?" Sundar asked.

The other sadhu winced. "That is my problem," he began. "I have been exercising this discipline for eighteen months, but I have not yet reached my goal. Indeed, it is not possible to find release in such a short time; it will take many years, even many lives, before I can hope for release from my sinful nature."

Sundar stood quietly watching the man, thinking about the empty promises of Hinduism. *How cruel it is to think that we must torture ourselves through many lives in order to find true peace. If we do not reach our goal in this life, why should there be another chance in another life? Is it even possible in thousands and thousands of lives?*

"Brother," Sundar finally said, "consider the notion that neither you nor I will ever find peace through our own efforts. I have found that peace is a gift from God, not the wages of self-denial and sacrifice such as you are making. Seek the life of God, and not the death of the flesh."

A little farther along the road, Sundar encountered another sadhu doing penance. His feet were tied with a rope, and he was hanging upside down from the branch of a tree. Sundar sat down under the tree and waited for him to finish his exercise. When he came down, Sundar asked, "Why do you do this? What is the purpose of such torture?"

"People are very surprised to see me hanging head down from a tree, but this is my method to serve God and do penance. When I am hanging upside down, I remind myself and others that all of us are bound by sin and lead lives that are, in God's eyes, upside down. I seek to turn myself upside down again and again until in the end I stand upright in the sight of God," the sadhu explained.

Once again Sundar struggled with the Hindu idea of penance. "It is true," he said, "that the world is upside down and its ways are sinful. But I ask you this: Can we ever hope to right ourselves through our own strength? Must we not turn instead to God, who alone can set right what is wrong and free us from evil thoughts and desires?"

The Hindu sadhu sat silently for a long time. "You have spoken wisely," he finally said. "I will have to ponder your words."

As Sundar continued his journey west, he prayed for the two sadhus he had encountered. It saddened him to think how earnestly they searched for peace of heart and failed to recognize that finding it was a matter of faith and not painful exercises.

Sundar continued to head west, and finally he climbed over the Khyber Pass into Afghanistan. He traveled on in Afghanistan until he came to the city of Jalalabad, where he stayed for several weeks and preached in the streets. But Sundar was now in an area where the people spoke the Pashtu language, and since he could neither speak nor understand the language, he decided to travel no farther. Instead he turned around and headed east, back toward India.

It was August 1906, and Sundar was in the town of Jammu in Kashmir, one hundred miles north of Lahore, when he noticed another sadhu in an orange robe. This man, though, was a European, and Sundar soon learned that his name was Samuel Stokes. Samuel explained that he had come from America to preach the gospel to the Indian people in the countryside and remote villages of the north.

Sundar was immediately intrigued to find a foreigner with the same calling as his own, and the two men soon decided to travel together throughout the fall and winter months. Their first night together turned out to be quite a test. No one in Jammu had offered them food or a room in which to stay. But as night fell, a farmer relented and allowed the two sadhus to stay in his cowshed. Sundar gagged as he entered the foul-smelling place. Still, it was all they had, and the two men thanked God for a roof over their heads. Later the farmer brought them a loaf of stale bread, and again they gave thanks to God. Because bugs and rats were crawling around, making it impossible to sleep, Sundar and Samuel spent much of the night talking and praying.

Sundar pointed out that the two of them were taking shelter in a stable, the same type of place where Jesus had been born. The thought cheered them, and Samuel began telling Sundar about another man, Saint Francis of Assisi, born in the twelfth century, who had wandered around Italy preaching and doing good to those he met.

"Saint Francis was born into a wealthy family. His father was a merchant," Samuel said. "As a young man his sole aim in life was to enjoy himself. He gained a reputation for throwing parties and telling the wittiest stories. Then, when he was about twenty years old, he became ill. During his illness he thought long and hard about what would happen to him if he died. And he came to the conclusion that he would not be worthy to go to heaven."

"So what did he do?" Sundar asked, brushing a spider off his arm.

"He renounced his father's wealth and took a vow of poverty. Then he went from town to town preaching and helping the people. He often worked with lepers, and over time other wealthy men and women joined him, which led to the starting of what would become known as the order of Saint Francis."

"How wonderful," Sundar replied. "To think that I am following in well-trodden footsteps. In my heart I thought that God might well have called other men at other times to do as I am doing, but I did not know for sure. And you, Samuel, have confirmed that to me. You will have to tell me more of this Saint Francis. I am especially interested to know how he balanced service to the lepers and solitude with our Lord."

Samuel nodded. "As we travel together, I will tell you all that I know of Saint Francis. Although I am a Quaker and he was a Catholic, he is my inspiration in coming to India. I, too, have turned my back on my inheritance and seek only to do the will of God."

During the night Sundar thought a lot about what Samuel had told him. Thoughts of Saint Francis inspired him to continue his journey, even though winter was coming and there had been little response to the gospel from many of the people in the villages he had visited.

The next morning the two men left Jammu and headed toward Kangra Valley. The weather grew colder, but they continued on, often traveling through the night, resting at dawn, and then preaching in the afternoons and evenings. Samuel had a "magic lantern" with him, which allowed him to project slides onto a screen or the side of a building. When he took it out, crowds would gather to view images of ancient Christian sites in Palestine and marvel at what they saw.

It was a long, hard, cold winter, and by spring both Sundar and Samuel were exhausted. Indeed, one day in a remote area, as the two young men walked along, Sundar collapsed at the side of the road. His body was wracked with pain, and he was overcome by fever. Because they were miles from the nearest village, Samuel left Sundar propped up at the side of the road and went to seek help for his traveling companion. About two miles away he found the house of an English planter, who offered to take Sundar in and help him. Samuel carried Sundar to the planter's house and placed him in bed.

Sundar's body was weak, and his recovery was slow. The planter insisted that the two men stay with him until Sundar was completely well. During the afternoons Sundar and Samuel would sit outside in the sun and talk to their host. At first the planter was not particularly interested in religious matters. But as their afternoons together rolled by, his interest was piqued. Soon the planter was asking probing questions about Christianity, and before Sundar was well enough to leave, the man had become a believer.

When Sundar's health finally returned, he and Samuel thanked the planter and went happily on their way. As far as Sundar was concerned, his bout of illness had been worthwhile, since it produced a Christian convert.

The two men headed for Sabathu, where they planned to spend a month helping in the leprosy hospital. Sundar was still a little weak, but nonetheless, when they arrived at the hospital, both men volunteered to do whatever they could. They were put to work changing bandages, bathing lepers, and cleaning the ward. It was dirty work, and they ran the risk of contracting the disease, but both of them worked wholeheartedly.

At the end of their month helping in the hospital, Samuel decided to return to the United States to recruit more Christian men to come to India and become sadhus. With Samuel's departure, Sundar decided to make a short preaching tour of the villages in the mountains around Sabathu.

One day as Sundar was leaving the village of Narkanda, nine thousand feet up in the mountains, he noticed that in a field below the village some farmers were gathering in their barley crop. He walked down the steep track that led to the field and greeted the farmers. But none of them seemed eager to greet him, especially when they learned he was a Christian sadhu and not a Hindu one.

"We don't have time for you," one of the men said. "Can't you see we are busy? Let us alone. We don't need your God. We need to get our crops in."

Sundar stood wondering how to reply to the man, when a rock hit Sundar on the forehead. The rock had been hurled at him by one of the other men working in the field. At first Sundar did not feel any pain, but he was aware that blood was pouring down his cheek. The rest of the farmers stopped what they were doing and watched, wide-eyed in horror. It was very bad luck to harm a holy man, Christian or not.

Sundar knew that the farmers were waiting for him to curse them, but instead he pressed the palm of his hand to his forehead to stem the bleeding. As he did so, he silently prayed, "Father, forgive them."

Sundar made his way over to a nearby stream and washed his face. Several sets of anxious eyes watched his every move. When they were satisfied that there would be no repercussions for the rock throwing, the men went back to the work of harvesting their barley. Sundar sat in the distance and watched them, waiting for the blood oozing from his wound to stop flowing.

About an hour later one of the farmers staggered over and flopped down beside the stream near Sundar. "My head," he gasped. "I have never had such a bad headache."

"What is your name?" Sundar asked.

"Nandi," the man replied.

Sundar knew that the other men would think he had put a secret curse on Nandi as a result of the stone-throwing incident, so he walked over to the field and picked up Nandi's scythe. Much to the amazement of the other men, he began swinging the scythe back and forth, harvesting the barley, and soon he was in a rhythm with the rest of them. He worked silently beside them until the sun set.

That night Sundar was invited to Nandi's house, where all of the farmers from the field gathered to hear him tell stories about Jesus Christ. Nandi insisted Sundar stay the night in his home, and the following morning he begged him to come back whenever he was in the area.

In the distance beyond Narkanda rose the Himalayan Mountains. In many of the villages he passed through in this area, Sundar had encountered Tibetan traders who had made their way over the mountains with trade goods strapped to their long-haired yaks. Their distinct flat Asian features and prayer wheels intrigued Sundar, who soon found himself once more thinking about Tibet. This strange land beyond the Himalayas seemed to be beckoning to him.

Chapter 7

Across the Mountains

In early summer 1908 eighteen-year-old Sundar Singh could no longer resist the feeling pulling at his heart, and he set out for Tibet. To get there he followed the Hindustani–Tibet road as it wound its way up along the Sutlej River gorge. It was a slow climb, but Sundar took his time, stopping along the way to talk to anyone he came across.

Along the road he met another sadhu, who was sitting surrounded by four fires as the sun blazed overhead. "Sadhu, you have a look of despair on your face. Why are you sitting amidst the fires on such a hot day?" Sundar asked.

"I am disciplining my body. I surround myself with fire all summer, and in the winter I stand for hours in the icy river below," the sadhu replied.

"And what have you gained from this discipline?" Sundar gently asked.

"Nothing," the sadhu replied. "I do not hope to gain or learn anything in this present life, and about the future I can say nothing."

Sundar used the opportunity to tell the sadhu how the God of the Bible offered him a life of freedom from sin through faith, not by strange and torturous acts such as sitting by a fire in the heat of the day. The sadhu promised to think about what Sundar had said and to read the tract he left with him.

The road ended at the town of Rampur, not the same town where Sundar had grown up, but another town called by that name. This Rampur was the crossroads between India and Tibet, and even the architecture was a mixture of Indian columns and the tiled, curved roofs of Tibetan homes. Tibetan traders, with their yaks in tow, were a common sight in town as they stopped to sell salt, yak butter, and yak-wool blankets that they had carried over the mountains. With the money they made, they bought grain and fruits and vegetables, which they took back to Tibet.

From Rampur the road became a yak track that wound up and over the Himalayan Mountains. Sundar, barefooted as usual and clad only in his robe with his blanket draped around him, hiked over sharp rocks and through the snow. Sometimes the passes he made his way over were more than twenty thousand feet high. As he climbed higher and higher, the air got thin, and he often found himself gasping for breath, but he kept on moving. Somehow he sensed that his destiny lay beyond these formidable mountains, and he would not turn back. His determination was rewarded when he crossed the main ridge of the mountains and began descending the other side. Sundar found himself in a place unlike any other he had visited.

As Sundar descended from the mountains, he was forced to ford many cold, icy rivers, and he traveled through areas where barely a house was to be found. But as he moved farther down the mountains, he began to notice clusters of mud-brick houses that clung to the sides of the steep ravines or were nestled beside the fast-flowing rivers. Long, colorful prayer flags fluttered in the breeze from poles on top of the houses. Yaks seemed to wander everywhere, as did children and men and women. The Tibetans were not at all like the people of India. Their faces were broad and flat and dark. Sundar soon noted that the color of their skin was made even darker by a layer of grime. Indeed, the only purpose the Tibetan people seemed to use water for was making tea—tea that Sundar soon discovered tasted foul to him. The tea was a mixture of rancid yak butter, salt, and boiling water. Each time he was offered a cup to drink, Sundar found himself praying for the strength to gulp it down.

Finally Sundar reached the village of Poo, where he had heard that two Moravian missionaries lived and worked. It did not take him long to locate the two men, Kunick and Marx, who welcomed him with open arms into their mission house. Over the next several weeks, Kunick and Marx taught Sundar the rudiments of the Tibetan language. But it was a complicated language, and Sundar was glad when the two missionaries offered to send an interpreter named Tarnyed Ali along with him as he traveled farther into Tibet.

Sundar and Tarnyed Ali set off together into the unknown. The Moravian mission was the last Christian outpost of any sort in the country, and as the two missionaries passed through villages, no one welcomed them into his home. Instead, the two young men spent most nights sleeping out in the open. Undeterred, they prayed together and hiked on. In one village, called Kiwar, as Sundar stopped to take his customary bath in a local stream, people from the village came running out, brandishing sticks and yelling, "Get away from us! The lama says you are not men of God. No man of God would wash himself."

Saddened by the superstition of the Buddhist lamas, who held great sway over the people, Sundar climbed out of the stream and walked away, Tarnyed Ali following behind. They were run out of the next village and the one after that as well.

Weary and now beginning to feel a little discouraged, Sundar and Tarnyed Ali found a disused hut clinging to the side of a mountain and went inside. With no windows, the hut was gloomy, and the air inside was thick with the smell of stale smoke. When Sundar touched one of the walls, he found that like in most Tibetan houses, it was covered in a layer of soot and grime. A small fireplace was in the center of the hut, and nearby sat a pile of twigs and several cakes of yak dung to burn. Tarnyed Ali set about building a fire.

The fire had just burst into life when Sundar heard a faint noise outside. As he listened, the noise got louder. Then he recognized the sound of footsteps. Perhaps the hut was not deserted after all.

The figure of a Tibetan man soon appeared in the doorway of the hut. The man seemed just as surprised to see Sundar and Tarnyed Ali as they were to see him.

"I am sorry," Sundar said. "We thought this hut was deserted."

"It is," the man said. "I stop here for the night sometimes when I am passing by."

"Then, please, join us," Sundar said, relishing the company of the Tibetan man. Perhaps this man would be more open to hearing about Jesus Christ than his fellow countrymen seemed to be.

"I am Norbu," the man said as he came in and plonked himself down on the ground across the fire from Sundar.

Sundar noticed that as Norbu's eyes adjusted to the dim light inside the hut, he looked startled.

"You wear the robe of a sadhu," he finally said.

Sundar nodded. "I am Sadhu Sundar Singh," he said.

Norbu's eyes lit up. "You are not the first Sadhu Singh I have encountered in these parts," he said.

Sundar was immediately attentive. "Are you saying another Sadhu Singh has been here?" he asked, wanting to make sure he had heard the man correctly.

"Yes. And like you, he had a Sikh name, but he was not a Sikh holy man. He was a Christian holy man."

Sundar could feel the excitement pulse through his body at this news. There was another Sadhu Singh who was also a Christian! "Please, tell me about this holy man," Sundar invited.

"I will tell you all I know of him," Norbu began. "His name was Kartar Singh. He was the only son of a wealthy Sikh landowner. Despite being a Sikh, Kartar could find no peace in his heart until one day someone told him about the Christian God. Finally Kartar found what he was looking for and became a Christian. His father demanded that he renounce his new faith, but Kartar refused, and his father banished him from the family.

"Alone and without food or money, Kartar began working as a laborer. Eventually he saved enough money to buy himself the saffron robes and turban of a sadhu, such as you wear." He pointed to Sundar's now worn robe and turban. "Tibet seemed to call to Kartar's heart, and he set out across the mountains. Then one day he appeared here among us in these parts. The people were not kind to him. They mocked him and chased him from their villages. But there was something about the man. No matter how much the people persecuted him, he did not strike back. He simply accepted the treatment he received and moved on to the next village."

Sundar shot Tarnyed Ali a knowing glance.

"Finally the patience of the head lama of the area ran out. He had Kartar arrested and tried for teaching a foreign religion," Norbu went on. "Since the Buddhist faith forbids the taking of a life, Tibetans have found clever and sadistic ways around this injunction. So when Kartar was found guilty, he was taken out, stripped naked, and sewn into a wet yak skin and left in the sun. As the skin dried in the sun, it began to shrink, slowly crushing Kartar. And so you see, it was the yak skin that killed Kartar, not the Buddhists who watched his death. For three days Kartar prayed and sang to God, and each day a crowd would gather to watch him suffer. They would cheer when they heard one of his bones break from the pressure of the yak skin. On the fourth day, knowing that the end was near for him, Kartar asked that his right hand be freed so that he could write in the front of his holy book. His hand was freed, and he wrote a verse in the front of the book. As the day worn on, Kartar got weaker. Then he spoke to the crowd. 'Are you standing by to see a Christian die? Come and look attentively, because death itself dies here. O Lord, into Thy hands I commend my spirit because it is Yours.' They were the last words that Kartar Singh spoke, and he soon died."

Norbu sat for a few moments and stared into the fire, as did Sundar, contemplating what he had just heard.

"There is more," Norbu said after a few moments. "The personal secretary of the lama, curious about the holy book, picked it up and took it home. He thumbed through the book, eager to find what it was that had allowed Kartar Singh to face death so bravely. And then the secretary began to tell others about what he had read in the Christian holy book. More and more people wanted to know about the contents of the book, and soon some were calling themselves Christians."

"What happened to them?" Sundar asked.

"Of course the lama was furious," Norbu said. "The killing of Kartar Singh was supposed to have been a warning to the people against Christianity, but now it was having the opposite effect. And the lama was even more furious when he learned that it was his secretary who was spreading this new religion. He had the secretary arrested and beaten cruelly. The secretary's mangled body was then thrown onto a garbage heap, where he was left to die. But the man did not die. He felt an unexplainable strength well up within him, and he was able to crawl away off the garbage heap. When his wounds were healed, he walked back into the town where he had been beaten and left for dead. The people were shocked and became fearful. They wondered what sort of power had given strength and healing to one they thought was dead. As a result of this incident, the man has been allowed to wander the countryside and preach in the villages unmolested by the lama or the residents."

"That is truly an amazing story," Sundar said. "Tell me, if you know, where is this man today? Is he nearby so I could meet him?"

"He is closer than you think, Sadhu," replied Norbu, and then with a dramatic flourish he added, "I am that man!" With that he reached into his small bag and pulled out a worn and tattered New Testament. "This New Testament was Kartar Singh's holy book. See, here inscribed in the front is the verse Kartar wrote before he died."

Sundar took the New Testament and read what Kartar had written. Tears welled in his eyes as he pondered the words. He marveled at the similarity between his story and that of Kartar Singh. The story of Kartar's faithfulness encouraged Sundar and made him even more determined to keep on preaching to the Tibetan people, even if it cost him his own life.

Following a night in the abandoned hut talking and praying with Norbu, Sundar and Tarnyed Ali trudged on. Sundar insisted on practicing the Tibetan language as often as he could, because he knew he would be back in the country many more times and wanted the freedom to talk to the people without having to rely on an interpreter.

The summer slowly faded, and the wind began to turn icy. Sundar realized that it was time for him to head back across the mountain passes before snow completely blocked his way. Sundar and Tarnyed Ali made their way back along the same route they had come, and once again Sundar was grateful for the hospitality of the two Moravian missionaries in Poo.

After saying farewell to Tarnyed Ali, his traveling partner for the summer, Sundar left Tibet behind and made his way alone along the Hindustani–Tibet road. Along the way he heard of a holy man who had taken an oath of silence. Sundar made a detour to the village where the man lived and went to see him. He was immediately impressed with the fact that this sadhu was a genuine seeker after truth. In his quest the man had not spoken a word for six years. Sundar was eager to question him, and the sadhu offered him a slate and chalk.

On the slate Sundar wrote, "Didn't God give us a tongue so that we can speak? Why do you not use yours to worship and praise the Creator instead of remaining silent?"

The sadhu thought for a moment and then erased Sundar's question and wrote, "You are right. I am sure God does want our praise, but my nature is so evil that I cannot hope for anything good to come out of my mouth. Therefore I have remained silent for six years. It is better that I remain silent until I receive some blessing or message that can help others."

Sundar then told him about Jesus Christ and how His death could change any person's heart from evil to good, but the sadhu wrote that he found the idea too simple to be true, so Sundar parted from him without a word.

A little while later Sundar stopped at the small settlement of Kotgarh, about twenty-five miles northeast of Simla. Although the settlement, located seven thousand feet up in the mountains, was nothing more than a handful of houses and some orchards and cornfields, it was set in the middle of a majestic pine forest. Sundar decided to stop and rest there for several days before continuing his journey.

On his second day in Kotgarh, Sundar met a man named Susil Rudra. Much to Sundar's delight, Susil was also a Christian, and the two men were soon lost in deep conversation. Susil explained that his father too had been a Christian. His father had come from a Hindu background and determined to stay as faithful as he could to that tradition, except where it conflicted with Christian beliefs. Many people, both Hindu and Christians, had found this difficult to accept, but Susil's father persisted. And now Susil followed that tradition. He explained to Sundar that he believed that the Christian church in India needed to have a distinct Indian identity rather than the English identity it had in so much of India. Sundar couldn't agree more. He and Susil forged a camaraderie in their desire to stay true to their Indian culture while at the same time being Christians.

Sundar learned that Susil was the principal of Saint Stephen's College in Delhi. This school, Susil explained, focused on giving young men from the Punjab region a Christian university education.

Susil had come to Kotgarh for a vacation away from the stifling heat of Delhi. Accompanying him was Charles Andrews, a British missionary who was a teacher at the school. Sundar soon found that he liked Charles very much. Charles was not like so many other English missionaries he had met before. Charles shared Susil's view that the Christian church in India should have a distinct Indian flavor. And he was quick to criticize those who tried to make it too English.

Over the next several days, Charles and Susil talked to Sundar about his future. "After all," they told him, "you are just nineteen years old. If you really want to impact the Christian church in India, it would be much better if you had some credentials. You need a regular system of Bible study, too. It is all very well for you to read the New Testament for hours on end, but there are many wonderful truths to be found in the Old Testament as well."

Sundar could see the logic in what they were saying to him, and so he agreed to allow Charles to enroll him in a two-year course at Saint John's Divinity College at Lahore. As he made his way there, Sundar had no idea how difficult this new direction would be for him.

Chapter 8

A Caged Forest Bird

It was New Year's Day, and Sundar stared at the mass of young men surrounding him at the dinner table. He had been at Saint John's Divinity College for three weeks now, and he wondered whether he and the other students had anything in common besides the fact that they were all Indians. He remembered the day he arrived at the school. Everyone else had boxes and suitcases, while he walked quietly in through the gates with nothing but the clothes on his back and his Urdu New Testament. Doting mothers and stern fathers who warned their sons to work hard and get good grades had accompanied the other boys. Sundar, on the other hand, knew that his father and brothers did not even know where he was and did not care. The comparisons did not end there. Most of his fellow students came from Christian homes. Attending Saint John's was a deliberate career choice they had made. Most of them hoped to be deacons and priests in the Anglican Church. But Sundar could not see himself fitting in to the restrictions of working for any single denomination.

In only three weeks he had become increasingly weary of the chatter at mealtimes, the games the boys played, and the lack of time for meditation and prayer. How Sundar longed for the mountains around Simla and Kotgarh where he used to pray for hours, sometimes days at a time, and read an entire Gospel in one sitting. He had to admit to himself that he felt lonelier at Saint John's among Christian students than he did when he was out trekking alone through the foothills of the Himalayas.

Sundar realized that the other students were not comfortable with a young sadhu in their midst either. Sometimes when he walked past a group of students, he got the feeling they were talking about him, and a small group of first-year students taunted him in the dormitory most nights. This group of students was led by a student named Prem. Sundar had no idea why Prem appeared to hate him so much.

Unable to finish his meal, Sundar slipped out of the noisy cafeteria. He wandered the school grounds for a while before finally sitting down with his back propped up against the trunk of a tree. With tears in his eyes, Sundar began to pray out loud. "O

Lord, sometimes I feel so alone, but I know that You are with me and You will see me through this dark period in my life. I pray for the boys here who taunt me, especially Prem. If there is anything I have done to offend him, please forgive me. I want Your love to flow between us, so show me if I am a stumbling block to my brother."

A branch cracked behind Sundar, and as he opened his eyes and turned his head to see what it was, he looked right into the eyes of Prem. The two of them looked at each other for a long moment, and then Prem fell to his knees.

"Forgive me, Sundar, please forgive me," Prem begged. "I am the one who needs to be forgiven, not you. I do not know why I have felt such anger toward you. It is certainly nothing you have done to me."

He put his head on Sundar's shoulder and wept.

"I promise I will never make fun of you again. In fact, I would very much like to be your friend. Do you think we could pray together sometimes?" Prem asked.

Sundar looked once again into Prem's now wet, dark eyes, which shined with sincerity. He nodded. "I would like that."

From that time on, Sundar and Prem became good friends, and their friendship helped to ease some of the loneliness Sundar had been feeling.

Although divinity school was still not easy for him, Sundar comforted himself with the fact that when he was finished, he would be an ordained

Anglican priest. Then he could preach not only in the mountains and countryside but also in the churches dotting the land of India.

Eight months into his education at Saint John's, Sundar discovered that his vision of future ministry was quite different from that of Bishop Lefroy, the Anglican bishop and principal of Saint John's. Bishop Lefroy had invited Sundar into his office for a chat. Sundar sat in a soft, leather chair opposite the bishop.

"So how are things going for you, Sundar?" Bishop Lefroy asked.

"Very good, sir," Sundar replied. "I must say that my time here has been more difficult than I had imagined it would be. But that is fine. It is worth the sacrifice so that I can become ordained and preach not only in the villages and marketplaces where people gather but also in the churches throughout India."

Sundar watched as a bemused look spread across the bishop's face.

"Sundar, let me explain," Bishop Lefroy began delicately. "If you are ordained as an Anglican priest, you will not be able to wander all over India preaching. As an ordained priest, you will have a church, or perhaps a group of churches, that you must care for. And you will have to remain in the diocese where you are ordained. You will not be free to travel to Bombay or Delhi or Calcutta or anywhere else to preach without the permission of the bishop of that diocese. I thought you understood this when you agreed to come here."

Sundar realized that he should have known this, but he did not. He felt a heaviness creep into his heart as he shook his head. "No, I did not know that," he said. And then he asked, "What about Tibet? Would you allow me to go there, since it is not under the direction of any diocese?"

After an uneasy moment of silence, Bishop Lefroy spoke. "Tibet belongs to no one, I will grant you that. But again, Sundar, you cannot just leave your diocese for four or five months at a time each summer to lose yourself in Tibet. As noble an aim as wanting to share the gospel with the people of Tibet may be, you will have a church full of people who look to you for spiritual guidance and leadership. You cannot just leave them when it suits you."

Sundar sat staring at the leather-bound books neatly arranged in rows on the mahogany bookshelves behind Bishop Lefroy and pondered what he had just heard. The life of an Anglican priest was not the ministry he felt called to. He was called to be a Christian sadhu, a missionary to the people of India and Tibet. He had hoped that being ordained might expand his ministry. He never imagined for a moment that it would have the opposite effect. Deep down Sundar knew that a theological education from Saint John's was not right for him, not if it hampered his ability to do what God had called him to.

"Bishop Lefroy," Sundar began as politely as possible. "I thank you for all you have done for me these past eight months, but I am afraid I must withdraw from Saint John's. It is clear to me now that my ministry is not compatible with the direction the Anglican Church would have me go in. I trust that in the future, when we meet again, we can enjoy wonderful Christian fellowship together."

"That we will, Sundar," the bishop said gently. "I am sorry that we have different views of the future of your ministry. I had high hopes that you would settle into a diocese and become a great pastor and positive influence on other ministers around you. But if that is not to be, then I pray God will bless your ministry. I wish you every success in the future."

With that Sundar stood and left Bishop Lefroy's office.

As Sundar walked out the gates of Saint John's Divinity College for the last time, he felt as though a weight had been lifted from his back. Once again he was free to go wherever he felt God had called him to and to speak to whomever he wanted along the way. One of the first places Sundar visited was Saint Stephen's College in Delhi. Susil Rudra and Charles Andrews, the two men he had met at Kotgarh, gave him a warm welcome. Charles, who had visited Sundar at Saint John's, told him how glad he was that Sundar had decided to leave. He explained that when he saw how unhappy Sundar had been at the divinity college, he realized the mistake he had made in recommending the place. He told Sundar that he had seemed to him like a caged forest bird that was used to flying wherever he willed.

Now that Sundar was a guest and not a student, he was free to talk to the Christian boys attending Saint Stephen's College and encourage them to follow Jesus' example of service. Susil and Charles were delighted with the effect he was having on the student body and invited him back to stay at the college anytime he was in the area.

A month after his visit to Saint Stephen's College, Sundar received a letter from Susil. In the letter Susil reported that the most extraordinary things had happened following Sundar's visit. Many of the boys took his words to heart, and the school had been transformed. One boy, Samuel, had decided to give up his hope of landing a good government job and to enter into full-time ministry in the church instead. Another young man, Theofilus, spent three nights nursing one of the school's sweepers, who had contracted cholera. Before Sundar had come to Saint Stephen's, Theofilus would not have even looked directly at the man because of his menial job. And Amrit Singh had returned from vacation carrying a lower-caste man on his back. The man was suffering from the plague, and Amrit had found him dying in a forest and decided to bring him back to the college to be taken care of properly.

Sundar was delighted and wrote back to say that he would visit again as soon as he could. Then he continued with his travels. Sometimes he was able to speak and preach the gospel openly to the people of the villages that he visited. At other times he was run out of villages where he sought to speak. Undeterred by the response of people to him, Sundar plodded on. He headed in a southeasterly direction and traveled as far as Benares, located on the banks of the Ganges River.

Benares was a city to which many thousands of Hindu pilgrims came to seek forgiveness by bathing in the water of the sacred river, known to Hindus as the Mother Ganges. There, at the Hindu shrines dotting the banks of the Ganges, Sundar found a ready audience of people to talk with. As happened in the villages, sometimes the people listened quietly to what he had to say, and at other times the crowds became agitated and abusive when they realized he was talking about the Christian God.

One day Sundar was speaking to a group of Hindus who listened respectfully to what he was saying. When he had finished speaking, several men in the group urged Sundar to speak to their holy man, who was sitting farther along the riverbank. They explained that although they did not have the knowledge to argue with Sundar, their holy man would soon prove him wrong. A young man ran off to get the holy man and soon returned with him in tow. The Hindu sadhu, an old man with a dark, weathered face, walked up to Sundar and stared him in the eye. Then he did something Sundar had not expected. Instead of refuting what Sundar had said to the group, the man stretched out two of his fingers and placed them first in Sundar's mouth and then in his own. The crowd gasped. This was not what they had expected. By his gesture the Hindu holy man was indicating that he and Sundar's words were the same. The holy man then turned to the confused crowd and declared that all Sundar had said to them about Jesus Christ was indeed true.

Sundar was totally surprised by the turn of events and could hardly wait to get the Hindu holy man aside and talk to him in private. When they finally were alone together, the holy man explained to Sundar that although from all appearances he looked like a devout Hindu, he was, in fact, a Christian. He belonged to a group of Christians called the Sannyasi, who did not openly declare their faith but rather lived as Hindus and privately shared the gospel with other Hindus when the opportunity arose. They even had their own churches, but these were disguised on the outside as Hindu shrines. Inside, though, were none of the Hindu idols that usually populated such shrines. But neither were there crosses or other Christian symbols to give away what the shrine was actually used for. In their disguised shrines, the Sannyasi practiced the Christian rites of baptism and Holy Communion.

As Sundar sat and listened to the holy man explain the ways of the Sannyasi to him, he was amazed, not only that they had been able to keep their group a secret right in the midst of the Hindu faith but also that a lot more Christian sadhus were in India than he had at first thought.

When Sundar finally left Benares and traveled on, he thought a lot about the Sannyasi. He admired and accepted the expression of their faith, yet at the same time he realized that being a secret believer was not the path for him. He had been called to publicly declare the gospel wherever he went, even across the Himalayan Mountains in Tibet.

Chapter 9

"You Are Alive!"

In late spring 1912 it was time for Sundar to set out for Tibet once again. This time he decided to follow a trail over the Kailas Range farther to the east from his previous crossing of the Himalayas. This region was where the Hindu gods were said to reside, and many Hindu hermits lived in caves amid the mountains. Many nomadic bands of robbers also wandered through the area, attacking and robbing Hindu pilgrims and Tibetan caravans. But walking barefoot and carrying only his blanket, Sundar must have seemed an uninviting target to them, and no robbers attacked him as he made his way past Lake Mansarovar. The lake was surrounded by mountain peaks, wild swans swarmed over the lake surface, and many crumbling Buddhist temples dotted the shoreline. After he had passed the lake, Sundar began the arduous climb up and over the mountain range. Eventually he crossed the main ridge and descended into Tibet.

After leaving the Kailas Range behind him, Sundar walked for many miles before he came upon a small village. He tried to talk to the people who lived in the village, but when they realized he was a Christian, they grew hostile. So even though his bare feet were bleeding by now, Sundar decided to walk on until sunset. He asked which way he should go, and an old woman pointed to the southwest toward a high mountain pass. Sundar trudged off in the direction she had pointed.

It was bitterly cold, but Sundar pressed on, reciting chapters of the Gospel of John to himself as a way of encouragement. After about two hours of walking, he realized that he had been tricked. This was not the way to anywhere. The trail ended at the bank of a swiftly moving river. The water was icy cold, and there was no way for Sundar to cross it.

Suddenly the enormity of what he was doing overcame Sundar. He sat on a rock beside the river and cried with despair. It seemed that no one wanted to listen to him, no one would help him, and no one would care if he died and his body was washed downstream.

A few minutes later he wiped his eyes and glanced across the river. On the other side was a man warming himself by a fire. This made Sundar feel worse. Now he was within sight of warmth and comfort but had no way of reaching it.

Sundar watched transfixed as the man stood up and walked toward the river. Then, without even slowing his step, the man waded into the current, first up to his knees, then to his waist, and finally to his shoulders. Within a minute he was standing in front of Sundar.

"Sit on my shoulders and do not fear," the man said, reaching down to grab Sundar by the hand.

A great sense of calm came over Sundar, who did what the man asked. The man was very strong, and once Sundar was seated on his shoulders, he did not hesitate as he reentered the icy water. He carried Sundar to the other side and gently put him down. Sundar shut his eyes for a brief moment of thankful prayer. When he opened his eyes, the man was gone. There were only rocks within one hundred yards of the river, and they provided no place for the man to have disappeared to. Nonetheless, the man was nowhere to be seen.

Sundar sat with his mouth open, wondering what had just happened to the man. He waited, but the man did not reappear. Eventually Sundar continued on his way, thanking God that He had not forgotten about him after all.

The reception Sundar received at the next village and the one after that was also hostile. Sundar decided that his reputation was spreading throughout the region. This belief was reinforced when villagers began hurling insults and rocks at him before he even started to preach.

Finally Sundar reached the village of Rasar, located on a high plateau. As was his custom, he made his way to the marketplace, where he began to preach. A crowd soon gathered, and much to his surprise, they listened attentively. Indeed, some of the people asked questions about what he was saying and seemed satisfied with his answers. Then, to Sundar's surprise, the mood of the crowd suddenly changed. Many people walked away while others began to yell abuse at him.

Sundar soon discovered what had changed the demeanor of the crowd—servants of the region's grand lama were stirring them up. Once the people learned that the grand lama was unhappy with Sundar and his preaching, they lost all interest in what he had to say. Moments later the crowd that was left separated as the monastery guard marched forward and arrested Sundar. Rough hands dragged him off, and he was taken before the grand lama.

"It is against the law to teach a foreign religion in Tibet. You have been caught in the very act of doing that," the lama snarled. "Do you have anything to say for yourself?"

"No," Sundar replied. There was no point in pleading innocence. As the lama had already pointed out, he had been caught red-handed preaching the gospel.

"Very well, your punishment is death," the grand lama announced.

As he was led away, Sundar wondered about his fate. Was he to be sewn inside a wet yak skin like Kartar Singh and left to be crushed to death, or did some other fate await him?

Sundar soon discovered that the Tibetans had other creative ways of slowly killing people. He was dragged to the edge of town, where there was an abandoned well. A key was turned in the lock that kept the cover over the well in place, and the cover was pulled back. Sundar was then hurled down the dry well shaft. He landed with a painful thud at the bottom and watched as above him the cover was pulled back into place and locked down.

The air at the bottom of the well was putrid, and Sundar gagged as he breathed it. As he felt around him in the dark, he learned why the air smelled so bad. He was not the first person to be thrown into the well to die. Everywhere around him were human bones and rotting flesh, all that remained of the previous victims. Sundar soon discovered that he could not move without brushing against human remains, and he began to despair. As he stood in the bottom of the putrid well, Sundar found himself wishing for the wet yak skin that had slowly crushed Kartar to death. Kartar's death out in the fresh air suddenly seemed to him a better way to die.

Sundar leaned against the side of the well and tried to pray, but he felt like his prayers were not even making it out of the well. Desperation and loneliness washed over him, and he wished for a quick death. But his wish did not come true, and by his third night at the bottom of the well, Sundar was so weak he could barely move. He knew that he had only a short time left to live, and he welcomed the approaching hour of his deliverance from his hellish surroundings.

Then above him Sundar suddenly heard a clinking and a rustle. It sounded like the lock on the cover over the well was being undone, and then he heard a shuffle. Someone was sliding the cover off the well. Or was he? Sundar wondered whether his weary mind was hallucinating. And was that really moonlight streaming into the well? Suddenly a rope with a loop on the bottom was being lowered into the well. Was it real? Sundar reached his weak and shaking hand out and felt for it. It was real. Mustering all his strength and concentration, Sundar put one of his legs through the loop and wrapped his arms around the rope. Moments later he felt himself being pulled up out of the well.

Sundar gasped in lungfuls of fresh air as he collapsed onto the ground. In his semiconscious state, he heard the cover being pulled back into place and the lock being snapped shut. He turned to see who had rescued him from the well, but nobody was around. Whoever rescued him had disappeared into the darkness.

The fresh air felt and tasted wonderful to Sundar as he lay there, but he knew he would soon be noticed. He stumbled to his feet and staggered off into the night, guided by the light of the full moon that shone above. Finally he found some bushes near a stream and crawled behind them and fell asleep. When he awoke, the sun was high in the sky and baking down on him. It felt so warm and good.

Sundar lay in the sun awhile longer, feeling his strength return before making his way to the stream, where he washed himself and his robe and turban. As he sat waiting for his clothes to dry in the sun, he prayed and thanked God for sending someone to rescue him from the well. He wondered what he should do next. His first inclination was to get away from Rasar as fast as possible. But the more he thought about it, the more he became convinced that that was not what God wanted him to do. It was too good of an opportunity to miss. So Sundar pulled on his robe and turban and headed back into Rasar.

The people in the marketplace were wide-eyed when Sundar began preaching there again. As far as they knew, Sundar was dead. How could he now be preaching to them once more? News traveled fast, and it was not long before the monastery guard came and arrested Sundar once again.

"How can this be?" the grand lama stormed. "You were thrown down the well and left for dead. Who rescued you? Who is the traitor among us?"

Sundar tried to explain his rescue, but he had been so weak and semiconscious that he had not even noticed who it was that rescued him.

The grand lama was determined to get to the bottom of the matter. If there was a traitor in their midst, then, he declared, he was going to find him. That was when one of the lama's officials stepped forward and pointed out that there was only one key to the lock on the well cover, and that key was still clipped to the lama's belt.

The grand lama suddenly looked alarmed, and Sundar thought he noticed terror in the man's eyes. The grand lama abruptly stopped questioning Sundar.

"Get out of Rasar," the grand lama ordered Sundar, "and never return here lest the power that protects you bring disaster on us."

Sundar left the grand lama's presence and walked out of Rasar, sure that his return to the town had had a profound effect upon both the grand lama and the people of the town.

From Rasar, Sundar wandered on from village to village preaching the gospel. But soon it was fall and time for him to return across the mountains to India before the winter snow closed the way.

Back in India, Sundar kept busy visiting villages around the north and north-central regions of the country. The work was exhausting, but he kept at it. At the same time Sundar read and reread the Gospels, and as he did so, the more he felt God was calling him to fast as Jesus had done after His baptism.

Sundar remembered a forest at Kajiliban where he had spent time in the past. It was a lonely place located along the banks of the Ganges River between Dehra Dun and Haridwar, and Sundar decided that it would be a perfect place to fast. He climbed aboard a train for the long trip to the forest. The train was overcrowded as usual, with the people who could not get inside the carriages sitting on top of them or clinging to the sides as they rolled along.

For part of the journey, Sundar sat beside an Englishman. The man introduced himself as Dr. Smith, and he and Sundar fell into conversation. As they talked, Sundar explained that he was going into the forest to fast and pray, and that he hoped to do so for forty days just as Jesus had.

Dr. Smith was astounded at this revelation and asked Sundar many questions about his health. Finally he said, "I believe you will not survive such a fast, and I urge you not to do it."

Sundar insisted that he had to undertake the fast because he felt that was what God wanted him to do. So the doctor made a different request. "Very well," he said, "if you will not take my advice, at least give me the names of some of your closest friends that I may keep in touch with them and assure myself that you are safe and well."

It seemed like a reasonable request to Sundar, so he wrote down the names of Susil Rudra, Bishop Lefroy, and several other men.

At the next station, Nimoda, Dr. Smith left the train, leaving Sundar to complete his journey alone. Sundar arrived at the station near the Kajiliban Forest on January 26, 1913, and clambered off the train. Clutching his blanket and his New Testament, Sundar made his way into the forest and found a quiet place to fast and pray among a dense thicket of bamboo. He then gathered forty stones together into a pile. He planned to roll one of the stones away from the pile each morning to keep track of how many days he had been fasting. Sundar then began his forty days of prayer and fasting.

Each morning as the early sunlight filtered through the trees, Sundar rolled another rock off the pile and then spent the day reading his well-worn New Testament, singing chants, and praying. Soon one day melted into the next, and with each passing day Sundar began to feel a little weaker. In fact sometimes he found it hard to concentrate, and occasionally he forgot whether or not he had rolled away a rock that morning. Finally, after twenty-three days, Sundar lapsed into unconsciousness. He lay amid the bamboo thicket, alone and hidden from sight by the thick vegetation.

The next thing Sundar knew, he was being lifted onto a stretcher and hoisted up onto strong shoulders. He again lost consciousness, until he was lying in a bed. He felt crisp, white sheets enveloping him and heard a soothing voice.

"Ah, you are awake at last, I see," the voice said.

Sundar lifted his head half an inch off the pillow and nodded. He opened his mouth to speak, but no words came out.

"Do not strain yourself, Sadhu," the voice said. "You have been on quite a journey. Some bamboo cutters found you in the forest and brought you by train to Dehra Dun. Then some Christians brought you here to Annfield by bullock cart. You are now at Pastor Dharmajit Singh's home. He is away, but I am his son, Bansi, and I will take care of you."

Sundar managed a weak smile.

"They knew you were a Christian because they found a New Testament in your pocket, but I must confess that I did not recognize you until I read your name inside the front cover. I heard you speak once and was greatly impressed with your message."

Sundar listened to Bansi, but the effort exhausted him, and he drifted off to sleep.

It was three weeks before Sundar was fit and healthy enough to travel again, and when he did, Sundar was in for a big surprise.

"You are alive! You are alive!" a man in the train station at Chandigarh yelled when he spotted Sundar. "You are Sadhu Sundar Singh, aren't you?"

"Yes, and as you can see, I am indeed alive," Sundar replied. "Why do you suppose otherwise?"

"A month ago I went to your memorial service..." The man stopped and looked at Sundar. "Are you sure you are Sadhu Sundar Singh?"

"Of course. What memorial service?"

"The one at the Anglican church here. Many people were there: Christians and Hindus, and the priest read a letter of consolation from Bishop Lefroy. Surely you have heard you are dead? Your obituary has appeared in every newspaper in India."

It took Sundar several more hours to get to the bottom of the story. He visited the church in Chandigarh where his memorial service had been held. After startling the vicar, he learned that Dr. Smith had sent out a peculiar telegram to the men whose names Sundar had furnished him with. The telegram read, "Sundar Singh slept in Christ. Signed Dr. Smith."

All that Sundar could conclude was that Dr. Smith, the man he had met on the train, had been so convinced that Sundar would die during his fast that he had sent out the telegram heralding his death. The whole situation astonished Sundar, who hurried to the Simla area to show everyone that he was very much alive and well and ready for his next missionary journey.

Chapter 10

Into Nepal

After assuring his friends around Simla and across northern India that he was alive and well, in May 1913 Sundar set out once again for Tibet. As he made his way toward a village located along the trail that led up to the Himalayas, Sundar noticed two men ahead of him in the distance. As he walked on, he noticed that one of the men suddenly fell down. By the time Sundar caught up to them, the man had been covered with a robe.

"What has happened to your friend?" Sundar asked.

"He stumbled and fell, and now he is dead," the man said. "What should I do? I have no money to pay for a burial, and I do not wish to leave him here for the jackals to eat."

Sundar was touched by the man's predicament and decided to hand over his blanket and the two small coins someone had given him before he set out for Tibet. "Here, take these. I know it will not pay for much, but it will help. May God comfort you," he said as he handed his belongings to the man.

The man was very thankful, and Sundar went on his way. He had nearly reached the village, when the man came sprinting up behind him. "He is dead, my friend is really dead!" he yelled, as he grasped Sundar's arm.

Sundar looked at the man strangely. "Of course he is dead. I saw him fall. What are you talking about?"

The man wailed. "You see, Sadhu, my companion and I have been together for many years. We each take turns pretending to be dead in order to get money from unsuspecting travelers. After we had tricked you, I uncovered my friend, but he did not get up. I shook him, and he would not wake, for he really was dead this time." The man's face was ashen by now. "Forgive me, Sadhu. Forgive me for tricking you. I have obviously incurred the displeasure of the gods."

Sundar reached out and laid a hand on the distraught man's shoulder. "My friend, what you did was wrong, and I am sorry that your companion has died, but let me tell you about One who is the Lord of life and death."

Sundar went on to share the gospel with the man. The man listened attentively, asking questions as Sundar spoke, and eventually asked if he, too, could become a Christian. Sundar led the man in a prayer. Following the man's conversion, Sundar sent him on his way to the town of Garhwal, where there was a mission station and missionaries who would instruct him further in his new faith.

Sundar continued on his way over the mountain pass that led to Tibet. As usual, his summer in Tibet was a mixture of being taunted and abused in some villages and listened to and questioned in others. He also had some unique opportunities to preach.

On one occasion, as Sundar was climbing over a mountain, he came upon a man praying in a cave. So as not to fall asleep while he prayed and meditated, the man had tied his long hair to the roof of the cave. Sundar walked into the cave and asked the man what he was doing.

"I have led a life chasing after worldly pursuits, Sadhu, but that has only brought me emptiness and has not calmed my dread of an unknown future. So I have come to this cave to forsake the world and search for the enlightenment that will take away my fears."

"And have you found what you seek?" Sundar asked.

"Alas, Sadhu, I have not yet found that which I seek. No relief or enlightenment has yet overcome my spirit."

Sundar then began to share the gospel with the man. A look of delight slowly spread across the man's face until he could not seem to contain his joy. The man untied his hair from the roof of the cave and jumped up.

"Now my soul is at rest!" he declared. "Sadhu, this Jesus Christ, make me His disciple. Lead me to Him."

Sundar led the man in prayer and explained to him more about Christianity. Before they parted, Sundar encouraged the man to go to the nearest mission station.

On another occasion Sundar had been chased from a village by an angry mob. As he fled the village, he began making his way along a narrow ledge, when he slipped and dislodged a large boulder. The boulder tumbled from the ledge and crashed to the ground, right on top of an enormous black cobra, crushing and killing it. A young boy nearby saw what happened. He ran to Sundar and explained to him that he had just killed the snake that had bitten and killed several residents of the village. People were so scared of the creature that they no longer used the track along the narrow ledge that he was following. The boy then ran into the village and told everyone what had happened. The residents of the village were so grateful that they invited Sundar back to the village to stay with them. This time they listened attentively as he shared his faith with them.

On still another occasion, Sundar was making his way over a steep mountain pass strewn with sharp rocks, when his feet began to bleed. As he sat down at the side of the road to bandage them, a man making his way over the same pass stopped to talk to him. The man introduced himself as Tashi and asked what it was that drove Sundar to walk in bare feet over such rough terrain. Sundar explained to Tashi about Jesus Christ and the gospel and his desire to share its message with as many people as he possibly could.

When Sundar had finished bandaging his feet, the two men walked on together. Tashi explained that he was a seeker of truth but found himself perplexed with more doubts than ever before.

When they reached his village, Tashi urged Sundar to stay with him and tell his family about Jesus Christ. Sundar stayed with Tashi for a week, sharing the gospel before traveling on to the next village. Two weeks later Sundar decided to return and visit Tashi. Much to Sundar's surprise and delight, Tashi announced that he and his family had become Christians. Now they wanted to be baptized. Sundar reminded them that this was a dangerous act—that there might be severe consequences when the lama learned what he had done.

Tashi explained that he had once served as the lama's secretary and enjoyed a warm relationship with him as a result. So he had already gone to the lama and told him what he wanted to do. At first the lama was not pleased, but because of his friendship with Tashi, he would allow him and his family to be baptized as long as they did not try to actively persuade others to join their new faith. Sundar was amazed at the lama's broadmindedness, and he gladly baptized Tashi and the eight members of his family in a nearby river.

Finally the shadows began to lengthen, and the chill of fall permeated the air as Sundar began the trek back over the mountains to India before winter set in.

Back in India Sundar stayed in Simla for several weeks before beginning a tour of villages in the northern region of the country. His successes in Tibet over the summer spurred him on. Everywhere Sundar went, he encountered people who needed to hear the good news that Jesus Christ was the only Person who could lift them out of their despair.

In May 1914 Sundar found himself preaching in an area he had never been in before on India's border with Nepal. As he made his way along, he felt strongly that God wanted him to cross the border and go and preach in Nepal. It would be a dangerous venture. Christians were even less welcome in Nepal than they were in Tibet. To make matters worse, to enter Nepal legally you needed a Nepalese passport, and it was impossible for a Christian to be issued such a passport. These obstacles notwithstanding, Sundar decided to go anyway. He bought as many New Testaments in Nepalese as he could carry and set out.

Sundar crossed the border into Nepal at a high pass where there were no soldiers or border guard patrolling and began his trek into the forbidding country. The journey was incredibly difficult. Sundar was so cold that his hands and feet swelled to three times their normal size, and he was constantly hungry and thirsty. Still he climbed up one mountain after another, descending each one and fording the icy, fast-flowing rivers at the bottom as he continued on his way.

To his surprise, Sundar received a warm reception in many of the small villages dotting the mountains. Most of the inhabitants of these villages had never seen a foreigner before, and they had certainly never heard the gospel. Sundar was grateful that the Nepalese language was much like Hindustani, which he spoke. He thus spoke in his native language to the Nepalese people, who understood most of what he said.

Eventually, toward the end of June, Sundar reached his destination, the town of Ilam, one of the largest towns in Nepal. A garrison of the Nepalese army was stationed there. Well aware of the risk he was taking, Sundar entered Ilam and began preaching in the marketplace. A crowd soon gathered around him, staring wide-eyed at this man who dared to come into their midst and talk about a God who had risen from the dead and was going to judge them all one day. As the people asked questions, the crowd grew to several hundred.

Sundar was explaining Jesus' death on the cross, when six soldiers burst through the crowd accompanied by a high-ranking officer.

"Who gave you permission to preach this strange God in our kingdom?" the officer bellowed.

The crowd cowered, but Sundar drew himself up tall.

"I did not come on anyone's orders, except those of the Head of all officers, the Raja of all rajas, and the Creator of all that is created," he declared.

The officer turned red with anger, but Sundar continued in a firm voice. "The one true God has called all nations to eternal life, but the Nepalese people are unaware of this wonderful fact, so I have come to tell them. This eternal life is possible because of the death of God's Son, Jesus Christ. If you will not have faith in Him, a day will come when you will stand before Him and give an account of your life, just as I am standing before you right now."

"Well, we will see about that later," the officer snapped. "But I can tell you what is going to happen to you right now. You are going to be put into our jail, and we will all see if your Christ will come to your rescue."

Sundar was not surprised. "I am not afraid of this imprisonment. If I had been afraid, I would never have come here in the first place. Though you nail my feet to a log so that I cannot walk, I will still be free in my soul. If you do that to me, I will consider my feet not on wood but on rock that cannot be moved."

"Do not talk anymore," the officer ordered, glancing around to see how the crowd was reacting. The people stood passively watching.

But Sundar continued. "As long as I have life in me and a tongue to speak, I shall not stop talking about my Christ. In custody or not, I am ready to give my life that you may hear the good news."

The officer grunted and turned to one of the soldiers. "I have heard enough. Take him away and throw him in jail."

"But, sir," the soldier said, "if this Christ-God follower enters our jail, he will pollute it."

"You are right," said the officer. "We would be better to be rid of him completely. Take him to the edge of our territory and send him on his way." Then he looked at Sundar. "I forbid you to ever enter this territory or the town of Ilam again."

Rough hands grabbed Sundar's arms, and Sundar was marched from the marketplace and taken beyond the city wall.

"Go and do not come back," one of the soldiers told him as he pointed to the south. "If you are ever seen in this region again, you will be thrown in jail."

Sundar walked on a mile or so and then sat down on a rock, wondering what he should do next. The people in Ilam had been attentive as he preached in the marketplace, and he was sure that if he could just talk to them a little longer, some of them would understand what he was saying. He had no doubt, however, that the officer and soldiers meant what they said. He would be thrown in jail if he returned to the town. But that was a consequence Sundar was willing to face. Suddenly he felt a peace come over him. If he was thrown in jail, that would mean he could spend many days or even months sharing with the Nepalese prisoners. Perhaps

God had sent him to Ilam to reach out to these people. With fresh enthusiasm, Sundar gathered his saffron robe about him and set out to return to Ilam.

A short while later Sundar was once again preaching in the marketplace at Ilam. This time, though, the people were more cautious about stopping to listen to him. Sundar was sure it was because they did not want to be arrested by the soldiers for showing an interest in this new religion that their leaders obviously feared and despised.

Sundar had been preaching only a few minutes when a group of soldiers surged into the marketplace and once again arrested him. This time they followed through on their threat. Sundar was dragged off to jail.

At the jail Sundar had his robe pulled off, and he was made to lie face down on the stone floor, where his hands and feet were shackled with chains. Then a soldier appeared in his cell carrying a large earthen jar. With a smirk he emptied the contents of the jar onto Sundar's back. Sundar gasped when he realized what the jar had contained—leeches. He braced himself as the creatures burrowed into his back and began sucking his blood.

The pain was excruciating, and Sundar found himself biting his lip as he silently prayed and asked God for the strength to bear the torture. But the leeches were not the only torture his captors had in mind for Sundar. Soon a mob of people, whipped into a frenzy by the soldiers, gathered outside the bars of his cell. They hurled abuse at him as well as garbage, rotten fruits and vegetables, waste, and any other vile thing they could get their hands on.

After two hours of abuse and torture, the pain of the leeches sucking blood from Sundar's back began to subside. A peace swept over Sundar, and he began to sing and praise God. At the sound of his singing, the mob grew and pressed harder against the bars of his cell. It was too good an opportunity to miss, so Sundar began to preach and tell the people more about Jesus Christ and the Christian message. No one hurled anything at him now, and a calm settled over the mob as they listened intently to the words of the man chained up in the cell in front of them. Sundar could see the confusion in their eyes and knew exactly what they were thinking, and he addressed their concern.

"I know what you are thinking," he said. "You are fearful and wondering what power it is that allows me to preach to you while my body is being devoured by leeches and you hurl all manner of vileness at me. That power is Jesus Christ, and I am privileged to suffer for Him."

Finally the soldiers had had enough of his preaching, and four of them stormed into the cell. Sundar could see fear in their eyes. Without saying a word, the soldiers unchained him and dragged him to the outskirts of Ilam. There one of the soldiers threw his robe and New Testament at his feet and once again warned him not to return to the town.

This time Sundar did not reenter Ilam. He knew that the people there had seen and heard the gospel that day. Instead, dizzy from the loss of blood caused by the leeches, Sundar staggered away from Ilam and began the long, weary journey back home.

Once he had crossed the border back into India, he met up with a man named Tharchin, a Tibetan Christian who had worked with the Moravian missionaries. Sundar was glad to see him. Tharchin bathed Sundar's leech-ravaged back with iodine and watched over him while he recovered from his ordeal in Ilam.

Even though Sundar was in severe pain for many days, he considered his first missionary trek into Nepal a success. Hundreds of people had heard about Jesus Christ for the first time, and he determined that he would return one day to continue his preaching in the country.

Chapter 11

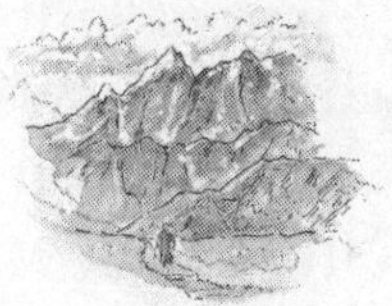

To the South

Christian men, both Indian and European, had often asked Sundar if they could accompany him on his missionary journeys into Tibet, but he normally turned them down. However, in April 1917, he set out from Dehra Dun for Tibet with four traveling companions, two Europeans and two Indians. The men planned to reach a barren area of Tibet known as Kailash. Their first stop, ten miles north of Dehra Dun, was Mussoorie. It was a steady climb there, but it was a lovely spring morning, and Sundar enjoyed the walk. However, when they arrived at Mussoorie, two of the men declared that they were exhausted and too unfit to go on. This surprised Sundar, as he felt as though he had been on short stroll.

The three remaining men, Alexander Judson, a schoolteacher, Mohan Lal, a leprosy-hospital chaplain and Indian Quaker, and Sundar, left the other two men and continued on with their trip the following morning. The terrain became more rugged as they climbed farther into the Himalayas. The temperature dropped twenty degrees as a severe storm blew in, dumping ice-cold rain down on them. Soon all three men were soaked to the skin. As they climbed higher, the rain turned to sleet, and then to snow. Despite the fact that Alexander and Mohan wore heavy, padded jackets and leather climbing boots, the two of them shivered with cold. They complained that their feet were numb, while Sundar's bare feet felt perfectly fine. Even when he caught his toe on a rock and it started to bleed, Sundar hardly felt it, because over the years his feet had become so hardened to walking.

Eventually Alexander and Mohan announced that they could not go any farther and begged Sundar to guide them back to Mussoorie. Sundar agreed; he could see that the men were in no condition to continue. When they arrived back in Mussoorie, Sundar offered to lead them into Tibet by a different, less arduous route, but the two men were much too exhausted to contemplate continuing.

The following day Sundar set off again for Tibet, this time alone. Soon another traveler, a Tibetan man, joined him, and the two of them walked on in companionable silence as they summitted the sixteen-thousand-foot-high pass, with its thin, icy air, and began their descent from the heights of the Himalayas.

Suddenly, halfway down, the weather turned bitterly cold. Sundar pulled his cotton blanket tight around him and picked up his pace, praying that he and his companion would not freeze to death along the trail.

As the two men edged their way forward in single file along a narrow, slippery ledge, Sundar looked down, carefully gauging each step. Far below, sprawled in the snow at the bottom of the ravine, was the body of a man! As Sundar peered at the body, he saw an arm move—the man was alive!

Sundar tugged at the fur jacket of his traveling companion. "Look down," he yelled into the howling wind. "A man has fallen down there. We must try to rescue him."

Sundar's traveling companion refused to help, protesting that they themselves would die if they delayed getting to the small village at the bottom of the trail. Sundar knew the Tibetan was right. On previous trips across these mountains, he himself had come upon the bodies of men frozen to death by a sudden change in the weather. But as his traveling companion continued picking his way along the ledge toward the village, Sundar stayed behind. He prayed out loud and then carefully began edging his way down the side of the ravine, aware that he was one careless move away from sharing the same fate as the man he was trying to save.

Finally Sundar reached the man and carefully lifted him onto his back. Then he draped his blanket around them both and tied the man to him like a baby to its mother's back. Through blinding snow and fading daylight and on bleeding feet, Sundar carried the man slowly but surely along the trail.

Then, as quickly as the snow had blown in, it stopped and the visibility cleared. It was then that Sundar could see the stone houses of the village a few hundred yards ahead. Relief overcame him. They were going to make it to safety! But his joy immediately turned to shock when he spotted the rigid body of his traveling companion who had gone on alone lying dead by the side of the trail, practically within shouting distance of the village.

Sundar said a quick prayer over the man and then staggered on the last quarter mile to the village. Soon both he and the man he had rescued were warming themselves in front of a smoky fire. As Sundar thought about the day's events, he realized that the exertion of carrying the man on his back and the contact of their two bodies had produced enough heat to keep both men warm—and alive. Sundar knew that if he had not stopped to rescue the fallen man, he, too, would most likely have frozen to death at the side of the trail with his Tibetan traveling companion.

The rescue marked the start of another long summer of witnessing from village to village in Tibet. News of the rescue quickly spread, and in its wake the hearts of many were opened to listen to what Sundar had to say, though others remained as hostile as ever. As Sundar approached one village, he decided to sit on a log and sing some hymns. He was halfway through his third hymn when people from the village began to appear from their houses and fields. One man, who was short but very strong, yelled abuse at Sundar. When Sundar did not respond, the man walked over and pushed him to the ground. Sundar put his hands out to soften his fall, but the jagged rocks cut one of his hands and his face.

Praying softly, Sundar unwrapped his turban and wound it around his cut hand. Then, with blood still running down his face, he sat on the log again and continued singing. When he was finished, he prayed aloud, asking God to bless everyone in the village and give them abundant crops. He then walked on, hoping to find a better reception at the next village.

As fall approached, there were no new converts, but still Sundar felt his time had been well spent. He once again made his way back across the mountain pass into India.

When Sundar got back to Simla, a huge pile of mail awaited him. In the pile was a copy of a Christian newsletter called *Nur Afshan.* The goal of the newsletter was to encourage Christians in northern India to live their faith openly. As Sundar skimmed through the publication, a letter to the editor caught his attention:

I am an employee of the Forest Department. In May, I was walking down a mountain road when I saw a sadhu with a blanket on his shoulder and a few books in his hand. I determined to follow him. The sadhu strode along till he reached a village. There he sat on a log and began to sing. When the village people realized that he was a Christian, they became hostile, and one of them knocked the holy man down, cutting his hand and cheek. The sadhu bound up his hand with his turban and continued to sing songs of praise to his God. When he left, he showed no signs of hatred. Instead he asked God's blessing on them all.

I stayed in that village and report to you that so great was the impression the sadhu made, the man who pushed him to the ground has already become a Christian and been baptized, and I am writing to you asking that your readers will pray for me, that I, too, might have the courage to openly confess faith in the Lord Christ.

Signed,
E. Das.

As Sundar read, he remembered the incident well and thanked God that his suffering had caused those around him to think about their own faith. For him two new Christians as a result of his efforts in Tibet made the hardships of the trip seem worthwhile.

Another letter in the pile of mail greatly surprised Sundar. It was from his father. It had been years since Sundar had heard from him. Sundar carefully read the letter, which opened with a general greeting, followed by a plea for Sundar to reconsider his future and come back to Rampur. Sher Singh wrote that he had a bride picked out for Sundar and spare rooms in the family compound for him to move into and start a family. With sadness Sundar put down the letter. He thought about how old his father must be now and wondered whether his father would ever understand the life that his youngest son had chosen to lead.

Other letters were also in the pile. Many of them were from people in western and southern India who asked Sundar to visit their churches and speak to their religious groups. As Sundar studied the return addresses, he was astonished at how far his fame had spread. One letter was from an Indian Christian he had met once before. This man said he had taken the liberty of writing about Sundar's life and teaching and had printed it in a booklet. He reported that the booklet was selling very well. Now Sundar understood why he was getting letters from all over India. People were reading the booklet and wanting to see Sundar in person.

The thought of traveling outside of northern India did not appeal to Sundar. He felt that his main purpose in life was to stir up Christians in northern India to make missionary forays into Tibet and Nepal. Anything else seemed like a needless distraction.

In December, though, Sundar reconsidered his resolve to stay in the north. He had traveled to the town of Baroda near the Gulf of Cambay and planned to return to Sabathu on the 5:00 AM train the following morning. He retired at nine o'clock and spent two hours in prayer, as he often did. While he was praying, Sundar felt that God was telling him that since he had already traveled this far south, it was time for him to go even farther south. The next morning Sundar did not head back north as planned, and at nine o'clock a telegram was delivered to the house. It read, "Please come to South India." It was the confirmation he had been looking for, and he bought a ticket on a train heading south.

Sundar had no formal plans. He trusted instead that God would guide him. As always, he carried nothing with him but his blanket, a New Testament, and a couple of books he was reading.

India is a huge, diverse country, stretching two thousand miles from north to south, and Sundar decided to travel down the west coast to the city of Ratnagiri. As Sundar made his way to the station to catch a train to Ratnagiri, he noticed on the ground a page torn from the Gospel of John. He bent down and picked up the page so that it would not be disrespected more by being trampled on. He folded the page in half and slipped it into his pocket.

Two hours later Sundar was sitting on the train, wending his way south. When the train stopped at a small station, a short man wearing a dirty robe climbed aboard and found a seat in the carriage not far from Sundar. As the train rumbled south again, Sundar was aware that the man had brought a strange, almost evil atmosphere into the carriage. He soon learned why this was. The man declared himself to be a sorcerer and began reciting chants and incantations. Before long he had put the man seated opposite him into a trance. It was then that Sundar decided he must act.

"You may be a sorcerer," Sundar said, "but I know One who is more powerful than anything you have experienced."

"Who is that?" the sorcerer snapped.

"Jesus Christ, of whom I am a follower."

Sundar noticed a grim look spread across the man's face. Then, with a flourish, the sorcerer leapt to his feet and moved to sit across from Sundar.

"Very well," the sorcerer said, raising his voice to be heard by as many people as possible in the carriage. "If you are His follower, then we shall see whose power is greater. I shall use my powers to subdue you and put you in a trance."

"You can try if you like, but it will do you no good," Sundar replied matter-of-factly, and then he said a quiet prayer under his breath.

For the next half hour the sorcerer focused all his attention on Sundar, chanting incantations and prayers as he tried desperately to put him into a trance. But Sundar remained wide awake and aware that everyone's eyes in the carriage were now focused on him and the sorcerer.

Finally the sorcerer looked up. "You have a book in your pocket that is preventing my spell from working," he declared.

Sundar reached into his pocket, pulled out his New Testament, and laid it on the seat beside him.

The sorcerer then went back to his incantations. But after a few minutes he stopped and said, "There is still a page of the holy book in your pocket that is blocking me."

Once again Sundar reached into his pocket, where he discovered the folded page from the Gospel of John he had picked up from the ground. He took it out and laid it on top of the New Testament.

Again the sorcerer went back to the task of putting Sundar into a trance. Once again he could not. This time he declared that Sundar's robe was impeding his progress, and Sundar took it off. Sundar sat clad only in a loincloth and turban as the sorcerer chanted more incantations. And once again the sorcerer failed.

"I see there is some mysterious power pervading you," the sorcerer finally confessed.

"You have spoken correctly," Sundar said. "It is the power of Jesus Christ, against which your evil is powerless."

Sundar went on to explain to the sorcerer the gospel and the power of Jesus Christ to change a person's life. The sorcerer, knowing he had encountered a stronger spiritual power, listened attentively to Sundar. The rest of the people in the carriage were quiet.

Finally Sundar arrived in Ratnagiri, where people were excited to see him. He soon found himself busy preaching to the crowds of people who flocked to hear him. At first Sundar was surprised by all the attention his presence in Ratnagiri had generated. He knew that news of him and his ministry had spread beyond northern India, but he had no idea that this many people were interested in what he did and had to say. Still he made the most of the opportunity to challenge the Christians who came to hear him with the need to go and preach the gospel to others. Many who came to hear him speak were not Christians, and a number of them were converted.

While in Ratnagiri, Sundar was invited to attend three choral performances by the girls at a Christian boarding school. The first evening, as Sundar sat outdoors listening to the girls sing hymns, he wrapped a thin scarf around his neck to keep warm. The following night, when he arrived for the performance, the girls presented Sundar with a thick, woolen shawl. Sundar was grateful for their thoughtfulness and generosity, and, with the shawl wrapped tightly about him, he sat listening to them sing.

Sundar used the shawl again the following night. When the girls' performance was finished, he began walking through the streets of Ratnagiri to the house where he was staying. Along the way he encountered a beggar shivering and trying to keep warm beside a meager fire. Without a second thought, Sundar slipped the shawl from his shoulders, placed it around the beggar man, and walked on.

The following day a special meeting was arranged for all of the lawyers in Ratnagiri to come to a local hall to hear Sundar speak. That night three hundred lawyers and their wives and children gathered. Sundar told them about his life and how things had changed so dramatically for him after he became a Christian. He then challenged his audience to follow his example.

At the end of the meeting, three of the lawyers prostrated themselves on the dusty floor in front of Sundar as a mark of respect.

"Do not do this," Sundar said, reaching to help the men back onto their feet. But as Sundar left the hall, the women and children crowded around him. Many of the mothers reached out and took his scarf and touched it to the heads of their children, while other women reverently touched his robe.

This troubled a missionary attending the meeting. When the crowd finally dispersed he asked Sundar, "Why do you allow the people to pay their respects to you in such ways?"

"I do not want their honor. They do what they do out of love for me," Sundar responded.

"Yes, but such honor belongs to Jesus Christ, not you," the missionary said.

Sundar looked at the missionary for a moment and then explained, "Well, Sahib, I shall tell you why I get it and why I accept it. My beloved Jesus went to Jerusalem riding on a colt. The people took off their clothes and spread them on the road. It was the colt who walked on the clothes, not Jesus. The colt was honored because he carried Jesus. I am like that colt. People honor me not for my sake but because I preach Christ."

The missionary nodded, looking satisfied with the answer, and left the hall.

Following a successful time in Ratnagiri, Sundar headed farther south. The first thing he noticed was how hot it was getting. Sundar was used to the much cooler temperatures of the Punjab plain and the Himalayas, where even if it did get hot, it was a dry heat and he could find respite under a shady tree. But in southern India it was hot and humid, and there was nowhere one could escape the oppressive clamminess. Indeed, Sundar explained in a letter to a friend in the north that he felt as though he were a dissolving lump of salt. He found that as a result of the heat, he had to rest more than he was used to. Still, he kept himself busy preaching the gospel to everyone he came into contact with.

In southern India Sundar encountered Christians from the Syrian Church. This church traced its history back to the first century, when, tradition said, Thomas, one of Jesus' original disciples, came to southern India, where he preached the gospel and eventually founded a church. Sundar was intrigued by the church's long history, but he was also disappointed at the way the church had lost sight of the message of the gospel. So at a meeting of young people from the church he challenged them:

> O young men, awake and see how many souls are daily perishing around you. Is it not your duty to save them? Be brave soldiers of Christ. Go forward in full armor. Crush Satan's work, and victory shall be yours.... [Christ] has given you a precious opportunity to be saved and to save others. If you are careless now, you will never get another chance, for you will never pass through the field of battle again. The day is fast approaching when you will see the martyrs in their glory, who gave their health, wealth, and life to win souls for Christ. They have done much. Oh, may we not blush in that day.

Sundar wondered how these young people would receive his message. He had his answer at the next meeting, where twenty thousand people turned out to hear him preach. And at a third meeting thirty-two thousand Syrian Christians came to hear him speak.

Finally Sundar made his way to Madras on the southeast coast of India, arriving there on New Year's Day 1918. Although he did not know anyone in the city, he was soon involved in a whirlwind of preaching and meetings. Many of these meetings were held in traditional churches, but wherever Sundar went, he seemed to attract a crowd. As a result he found himself also preaching under palmyra trees, in village squares outside Hindu temples, and on dry riverbeds. At these venues anywhere from five hundred to ten thousand people would gather to hear him speak.

People seemed particularly struck with the simple illustrations Sundar drew from nature to illustrate his points. In one sermon Sundar told his audience that they could not deal with sin simply by cleaning up the outer practices in their lives. He illustrated the point by saying, "In every home there are spiders. Many of us, trying to get rid of sin, are like housewives who destroy the spiders' webs without destroying the spiders."

At another meeting someone in the audience asked him, "How can my poor prayers help anyone when I am so sinful?" Sundar replied, "The sun draws salt water from the sea, yet when it falls again to the earth, the water is clear and pure and drinkable. The sun has cleaned it. So it is with God and our prayers."

After each of the meetings, a throng of seekers followed Sundar, asking questions and begging to hear more about Jesus Christ. Sundar did his best to speak with them all. And it was not uncommon for him to be awakened in the middle of the night by some prominent Hindu man who wanted to talk about Christianity but was afraid to be seen speaking publicly to a Christian sadhu. Sundar welcomed such men into his room and answered whatever questions they posed.

It was not only seekers wanting to know more about Christianity that kept Sundar awake other nights. Sundar often spent the night in prayer, gathering spiritual strength for the following day.

Sundar's simple and straightforward style of preaching and living not only drew crowds to hear him speak but also attracted the attention of the news media. While Sundar was in Madras, a reporter from the local newspaper attended one of his meetings. The following morning Sundar's host read to him from the newspaper what the reporter had said of the meeting. According to the reporter, Sundar was

> a tall young man delivering his message with the fire of a prophet and the power of an apostle. The audience hung on his lips, and never for a moment allowed their eyes to stray from the central figure. The Sadhu was unlike all mental pictures formed of him—he was incomparably superior to all I had thought of him. As I heard the sweet words issue from the lips of the Sadhu, who stood before me a visible symbol of the spiritual culture of the East, set aglow in the resplendent light of the Gospel—a vessel of eastern art and beauty chosen by the Lord, and filled with His Spirit—my skepticism vanished like clouds before the rising sun, and the dreams of my life seemed to touch the borders of the real. The problem of Christianity in India is solved, and the Sadhu has solved it.

Sundar felt himself blush as the newspaper article was read to him. He certainly did not see himself in those terms. He was simply a young man obeying the call he felt God had placed on his heart. And he told his host, "I seek to draw no man to me, only to reveal to them a glimpse of the Lord I serve. Jesus told His disciples, if they would lift Him up from the earth, He would draw all men unto Him. Praise God that is true."

As his stay in Madras drew to a close, Sundar expected to return to northern India, where it was time to prepare for crossing into Tibet for another summer among the Tibetan people. But those plans had to wait. Still more people in southern India and beyond wanted a chance to see and hear Sadhu Sundar Singh.

Chapter 12

To Tibet Once Again

With so many people wanting to meet him and hear him preach, Sundar spent the next four months traveling to Vellore, Trichur, Calicut, and various small towns in southern India. At the end of this time Sundar was exhausted. He felt like every ounce of strength had been sucked out of him, and he gratefully accepted the invitation of a Christian lawyer to spend a month in solitude in his summerhouse in the mountains.

While at the summerhouse, Sundar spent several hours each day teaching himself English from a book. He realized that one of the most tiring aspects of preaching in the south was speaking in Hindustani and then waiting while it was translated into Tamil or one of the other languages of southern

India. Many people in the south spoke English, and Sundar longed for the day when he would be able to talk directly with them. Even if he could not, it would be much easier to find a translator to put his English into another language than one who translated from Hindustani.

At the summerhouse he also caught up on his correspondence. Many of the letters Sundar received were heartening. One read, "Ever since you left Calicut, I have been looking back with gratitude on those blessed days you spent with us.... We are again reminded of those days when last week a Mohammedan young man came to us and said he had decided to become a Christian as the result of listening to you."

Another letter from Calicut reported, "When you were in Calicut the sub-postmaster heard you, or heard God's voice through you. Some days after, he saw Christ calling him in a dream. He comes every day to read with me. He says he wants to be baptised and fully follow Christ."

As people in the surrounding area learned that Sundar was staying nearby, they began to visit the house, either to ask questions or just to get a glimpse of him. One man who came was a magistrate. He was very troubled, and Sundar invited the man to sit with him in the back garden. The two of them started talking, and the magistrate said, "Sadhu, I know your time is valuable, and I do not want to take up too much of it. I have spent my life studying religions, and there is one problem which none of them can answer. I would like your opinion on in it."

"Ask your question," Sundar replied, "and I will tell you if my Lord Jesus has given me any light on the subject."

The magistrate continued. "Every day thousands of men are born and every day thousands of them die. What is the profit of all this to God? I am inclined to believe that there is no meaning in it but that the various elements come together and then get dissolved as one of the processes of nature."

Sundar thought for a moment and then replied, "Sahib, you are a learned man, and I am not. I am not sure I can satisfy you, but with the little grace God has given me, I shall try to answer your question. Once I was sitting in meditation on a hill for some months. In the valley below I saw busy farmers at work, day after day. First I watched them plough the fields; then they manured them. When the rains came, they sowed seed. The seeds came up, and the plants grew. The farmers watered the plants and weeded them. The corn plants produced ears, then blades, and then full corn. As the corn ripened, the farmers took turns walking the fields at night, making sure that no wild animals or men ate the nearly ripened corn.

"Then one day the care of the corn was over. The farmers brought their scythes and began cutting the sheaths of corn, which they had so carefully tended all those months. The plants could have well asked, 'What is the profit of all this? Why did the farmers take such good care of us, only to cut us down in the end like this?'

"But you see, my friend, the plants did not know what the farmers knew. We may not know why we are born and why we die, but God does."

The magistrate nodded. "You have spoken well, Sadhu, and given me much to think about."

That night, and for many nights afterward, Sundar prayed that the magistrate would come to understand that God knew the reason why he had been born.

After six weeks of rest, Sundar received an invitation from a Methodist minister to come to Ceylon to preach. A ticket for the short voyage to Ceylon was included with the invitation, and Sundar decided to go.

At Uduvil, in Ceylon, the struggling American Methodist mission had built a special shelter of coconut fronds and had sent out invitations for people to come and hear Sundar preach. When Sundar arrived at the place, he found two thousand people waiting for him: adults and children, Christians, Hindus, and Buddhists, all of whom wanted to hear his message.

Each successive meeting in Ceylon attracted larger and larger crowds, and many people compared Sundar to Jesus and His wandering ministry. A group of young men followed Sundar from one preaching spot to the next, asking him questions and wanting him to pray for them.

Once, as Sundar sat meditating under a tree, a nobleman approached him. "Sadhu, you are the one all India is interested in. May I sit and talk?" the nobleman asked.

"Most certainly," Sundar replied.

The nobleman took a place on the ground and sat cross-legged opposite Sundar. "You have proved that you can draw men of every faith to you," the nobleman went on. "And you have shown that there is a measure of truth in every religion, that all roads lead to God. The Emperor Akbar built a great temple to all religions four hundred years ago. And the founder of your Sikh religion, Guru Nanak, discovered truth among the Hindu and Muslim faiths. But the time has come for another prophet, a guru who will draw all India to his feet. There are errors that must be purged from all religions so that the real truth might come forth. What is needed is a teacher who can unite the best of all religions and discard the unworthy. Jesus in this new religion would be the greatest revelation of God the world has ever seen, though Hinduism, Islam, and Buddhism would not be discredited or discarded. And you, Sadhu Sundar Singh, would be the prophet of this new way of Jesus. You would go down in history as a greater prophet than Guru Nanak, the holy men of Hinduism, even Mohammed."

Sundar sat and stared at the nobleman for a long time. Finally he said, "You have been sent to try me, to tempt me by appealing to my pride. But your scheme will not work. If you truly knew me and the things I teach, you would surely know that I teach and preach only Jesus. He is the one and only true manifestation of God. He is the only one who can lead men to new life and enlightenment in God. All these other religions you speak of will surely pass away, but Jesus Christ shall remain forever. I serve only Him, and I seek no glory for myself. I do as He leads me to do, and I count it a joy to suffer the privations of life in serving my Lord. Now go, for your temptation has no power over me. I am content with the lot the Lord Jesus has given me, and I seek no other glory but His."

With that the nobleman scrambled to his feet without saying a word and left. Sundar continued to sit under the tree until dark, thinking about pride and how easily it could enter his heart and turn him from his mission if he did not constantly stand guard against it.

Sundar returned to India from Ceylon in July and traveled northwest to Bombay to attend a conference. Following the conference he headed east to Calcutta. When he arrived there, he came down with a serious case of influenza, the same strain of influenza that had begun sweeping the world following the end of the Great War in Europe, leaving millions of people dead in its wake. Even so, Sundar was not afraid. Instead he prayed and committed himself into God's hands. And although he became very sick, he did not die. As he recovered from the illness, he continually thanked God for the opportunity for a long rest and more time to pray.

As much as Sundar would have liked to return to the Himalayan region once he had recovered from his bout of influenza, he felt God was calling him to go still farther afield. This time his destination was Burma, on the eastern side of the Bay of Bengal. To get to Burma, Sundar made his first major sea voyage. He enjoyed the experience. Being out of sight of land and surrounded by sea was a very different sensation from climbing over the high, rocky peaks of the Himalayas to get were he wanted to go.

Sundar arrived in Rangoon, Burma, refreshed and ready to preach. Bishop Lefroy had preceded him there and set up a series of meetings under the auspices of the Anglican Church. Just as in southern India, these meetings were hugely popular and attended by ever growing crowds.

After one of the meetings, an Indian man approached Sundar. "You do not recognize me, do you, Sadhu?" the man asked.

Sundar took a good look at the man and realized that he was the doctor who had treated him after he had been poisoned by his brothers. "Of course I do," Sundar replied. "You are the doctor who attended me in Rupar. What brings you here today?"

The doctor beamed. "I laughed when you told me about the resurrection of Jesus and that His power could heal you, but then I saw you recover from imminent death. When you left, I purchased a Bible and began to read it, and soon after I became a Christian. I live here now in Burma, where I am a missionary doctor."

Sundar reached out and embraced his new friend in Christ. It was one of the happiest reunions of Sundar's life, and he thanked God for using such a horrible situation to bring another person into His kingdom.

The meetings in Burma continued, and as a result, many Burmese people were able to hear the gospel clearly presented for the first time in their lives. Sundar was so encouraged by the response of the people on this side of the Bay of Bengal that he decided to continue his tour on to Singapore.

In Singapore Sundar faced a new challenge. For the first time he could not find an interpreter to take his Hindustani words and translate them into the local languages. This was discouraging, until he decided that it was a God-given opportunity to overcome his fear and begin preaching in English. At first Sundar felt that his words were awkward and slow, but with each successive sermon, his grasp of the language improved until he felt quite comfortable speaking English. This was heartening for Sundar, since English was the international language of Asia.

Encouraged by the success of his preaching in Singapore, Sundar decided to continue north up the Malaya peninsula to the island of Penang, where he had the unexpected joy of talking to a group of Sikhs who had been invited to hear him preach at Saint George's Chapel. At the close of the meeting, a Sikh man stood and invited Sundar to speak at the Sikh temple.

Other people in Penang were greatly touched by Sundar's simple message. The chief of police came to hear him preach and then gave a half day off to his police staff so that they, too, could go and hear Sundar speak.

From Penang Sundar made his way back to Singapore, from where he traveled on to Japan at the request of a Japanese bishop.

The crowds in Japan who came to hear Sundar speak were smaller than those in other parts of Asia, but Sundar did not care. He preached in Kobe, Osaka, Kyoto, and Tokyo, trusting that God was bringing the right people to hear his message.

Still awed at the places where he had been privileged to preach, Sundar left Japan for China, where he spoke at meetings in Shanghai, Nanking, Pastringfu, and Peking. Everywhere he went, people begged him to stay longer, and he became embarrassed by the things that were written about him. He read one newspaper article that said,

> His coming was most timely, and I trust has given the Peking Cathedral congregation a great lift. It was good to see a Methodist translating for the Sadhu in the Cathedral. It was fuller than it ever has been on a Sunday, and at the Monday meeting—a suddenly announced service—the Cathedral was again

full. His way of putting things in English is after the model of the Gospels.

In both Japan and China Sundar was impressed at the number of people who became Christians as a result of his preaching. He decided that this was because neither nation was burdened with a caste system like the one that dominated Indian society. Without such a system, people were free to make their own decisions. Sundar grieved at what a crippling effect the caste system had in his homeland.

From China Sundar had hoped to travel into a different part of Tibet, but at the time the Chinese and Tibetans were fighting each other, and he realized he would have to reenter Tibet by way of India.

On his return to India, Sundar spoke at a hurriedly arranged meeting in the memorial hall at Madras. News of his return from abroad spread like wildfire, and four thousand people turned out at the first meeting to hear Sundar preach. Sundar chose for his sermon the text "And ye shall be witnesses unto me both in Jerusalem...and in Samaria, and unto the uttermost part of the earth" (Acts 1:8).

When he had finished describing some of the experiences from his recent trip, Sundar concluded his sermon by saying, "I am going to the hills and to Tibet now. It is quite uncertain whether I shall be able to return, so serious are some of the risks attending the journey and my work in the region beyond. Even if I do not see you again in this world, I hope to meet you in heaven amidst the revelation of a new life and its surroundings. I wish you good-bye till we meet again."

As Sundar made his way from the pulpit a man thrust a bag of coins into his hands. Sundar immediately handed the bag back. "Brother," he said, "God has called me to a life of poverty and dependence upon Him. Just as Jesus told His disciples to go out without a purse, so He has commanded me." The man looked shocked as Sundar left him standing holding the bag of money.

But the man was not ready to take no for an answer and followed Sundar to the train station. As the train carrying Sundar pulled out of the main station in Madras, the man pushed the bag through the window. "This is for you!" he yelled as the train moved away, soon too far from the station for Sundar to return the money.

At the next station Sundar, taking the bag of coins, clambered off the train and went in search of a beggar. When he found one clad in rags, he dropped the bag into the beggar's bowl. The beggar looked amazed as he loosened the bag's strings to see what was inside. He then bowed to kiss Sundar's feet, but Sundar motioned for him not to. "Freely I have received, and freely I share," he told the beggar with a smile before climbing back aboard the train for the continuation of the journey north to his beloved mountains.

Although Sundar was eager to get back to Tibet, he was laid up for some time in Kotgarh while he waited for his cut and wounded feet to heal. Once they had healed sufficiently, Sundar set out with a Tibetan Christian named Tnaniyat.

The two men began the steep climb up and over Hangpu La Pass. It was a difficult crossing, which Sundar described in a journal.

> At a height of 16,000 feet we slept out on the open plain when the cold was so intense that all feelings went out of the body and we became numb all over. The whole of one night the rain fell in torrents and in the bitter cold we had to sit all night under an umbrella. This place is a very dangerous one, for many people have died in the snow.
>
> On the 15th of July we came to Hangpu La Pass, which is nearly 19,000 feet high, where we saw the corpses of three men who had died from the terrific cold. At this great height we could scarcely draw our breath, our heads and lungs were filled with pain, and the beating of our hearts sounded in our ears. Here is a great glacier in which many people have lost their lives, and their bodies have never been recovered to this day. Thanks be to God we passed through this awful place in safety.

The following day Sundar and Tnaniyat descended the mountain pass into Tibet, until they arrived at the small village of Mudh, where the headman of the village invited them into his house.

The village's headman also invited a prominent lama to dine with them that evening, and Sundar marveled at the openness of the lama. Most Tibetan lamas he had encountered in the past were more than eager to pass a death sentence on him or mete out some horrible punishment, but this lama was open and asked Sundar question after question about Jesus Christ and what it meant to become a Christian.

The surprising openness of the lama was reflected in the attitude of the people in other villages they visited. This time, instead of being run out of most villages, Sundar and Tnaniyat were invited to stay in the village and eat and talk with the people. The trial on this trip proved not to be the reaction of the people but the terrain the two men had to cross to get from one village to another. There were no roads to follow, just narrow, poorly defined tracks that often petered out. And there were countless rivers and streams to cross, and no bridges on which to cross them. Instead Sundar and his companion had to wade through the icy, fast-flowing water, which often came up to their chests.

Once as Sundar was attempting to cross the Morang River alone, his body became so stiff and numb that he could not bend and expend the needed energy to pull himself up onto the rocks on the far side of the river. Sundar had prepared himself to drown, when somehow on his third attempt to crawl out of the river he managed to hook one of his legs over a boulder and somehow roll up onto it out of the water. There he lay until he had warmed up enough to clamber up the riverbank and continue his journey on to the next village.

In these remote regions Sundar often encountered Tibetan hermits, men who had locked themselves away from the outside world in monasteries and caves. The hermits inhabited rooms where the sun did not penetrate and which they never left. In the confines of these rooms, cut off from the outside world, they prayed and meditated and twirled their prayer wheels.

Sundar longed to talk to these hermits about the true path to salvation, and one day such an opportunity presented itself. He was making his way across some mountains when he came upon an old Buddhist lama who lived in a cave. The man had closed off the entrance to the cave by building a stone wall, leaving only a small opening for air. He never left the cave and lived only from the tea and roasted barley that devout people brought and passed to him through the small hole. Because he had lived so long in complete darkness, the man had become blind.

When Sundar came upon him, the hermit was praying aloud. Sundar waited patiently until he was finished. Then through the hole he asked, "May I speak with you?"

It was too dark inside to see the hermit, but the man did answer. "Yes, I welcome conversation with fellow seekers," he said.

Sundar asked him, "What have you gained through your seclusion and meditation? The Buddhist religion teaches nothing about a God who hears our prayers. To whom do you pray, then?"

The hermit answered, "I pray to Buddha, but I do not hope to gain anything by praying and by living in seclusion. Quite the opposite, I seek release from all thought of gain. I seek *nirvana,* the elimination of all feeling and all desire—whether of peace or of pain." He paused for a moment before going on. "But still I live in spiritual darkness. I do not know what the end will be, but I am sure that whatever I now lack will be attained in another life."

"Surely," Sundar countered, "your longings and feelings arise from the God who created you. They were surely created to be fulfilled, not crushed. The destruction of all desire cannot lead to release but only to suicide. Are not our desires inseparably intertwined with the continuation of life? Even the idea of eliminating desire is fruitless. The desire to eliminate all desire is itself a desire. How can we find release and peace by replacing one desire with another? Surely we shall find peace not by eliminating desire but by finding its fulfillment and satisfaction in the One who created it."

The hermit replied, "We shall see what we shall see."

Finally it was time to return back across the mountains to India. The return journey was just as dangerous as the trek into Tibet had been, but Sundar made it safely back to Simla. From there he set out on a winter preaching tour of the towns and villages across the Punjab plain. He went as far east as his home village of Rampur, where a wonderful surprise awaited him.

It had been fourteen years since Sundar had last seen his father. Throughout that time he had not ceased to pray that somehow Sher Singh would become a Christian. With trepidation Sundar made his way to the family compound in Rampur. He still vividly remembered the terrible reception he had received from his father and brothers on his last visit and hoped things would be different this time. With tears running down his face, Sher Singh warmly welcomed Sundar into the compound. Sundar could see that there was something different about his father. But it was not until the two men were seated in the shade of a veranda and sipping tea that Sher Singh finally told his son that he, too, had become a Christian about a year before. He explained how he had been keeping track of Sundar's travels through reports in the newspapers.

Tears welled in Sundar's eyes as he received this news. After so many years of praying, God had finally answered his prayers, and he was once again sitting with his father, both of them now Christians.

The following day Sundar's father said to him, "Son, I know I have often told you that I disinherited you, but that was to try to get you to denounce your religion. The fact is that secretly I have always kept your inheritance for you. I want to give you a portion of it now so that you can travel freely around the world preaching the gospel to all nations."

Chapter 13

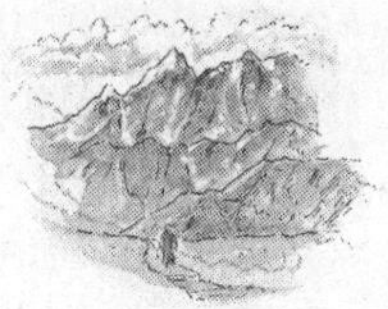

To the West

Sundar stood on the deck of the steamer *City of Cairo,* watching as Bombay and the west coast of India receded from view. It was January 16, 1920, and he was on his way to England. The voyage took over three weeks, and Sundar spent much of the time in his cabin praying about the speaking tour ahead of him. He was not sure what form it would take. All he knew was that meetings had been arranged for him in England.

The *City of Cairo* berthed at Liverpool on February 10, and members of the Society of Friends, or Quakers, as they were commonly called, met Sundar at the dock. Sundar felt immediately at home with these people, as they often worshiped in silence as he did. Even though it was late winter in

England, Sundar refused to wear shoes or an overcoat until someone pointed out that his muddy feet inconvenienced his hosts, who had to provide water to wash his feet before he could enter their homes. His hosts also pointed out that arriving at a person's home in a wet robe was not considered good manners in England. So, to be a better guest, Sundar bought himself a pair of sandals and a gray overcoat.

Try as hard as he might to remember, Sundar often forgot to wear his overcoat. On one particularly foggy morning he was standing on a busy corner waiting to cross the street when out of the fog a woman's hand appeared, clasping a letter. The woman started poking at Sundar, who immediately realized that she had mistaken the orange glow of his robe for a red mailbox. Sundar took the letter from the woman and said, "Ma'am, I would be very pleased to post that for you." He could hardly stop himself from laughing at the thought of how surprised the woman must have been to encounter a talking mailbox.

The Quakers took Sundar south to Birmingham, where he spoke at the Friends' Missionary Training College. He was still frustrated by his limited vocabulary when he had to speak, but he pushed himself to improve his English.

From Birmingham, Sundar traveled to the university town of Oxford, where he was invited to stay with an Anglican brotherhood called the Cowley Brothers. Sundar had met some of the men of the brotherhood in India and been impressed by their simple way of living. While in Oxford he was invited to carry out a series of lectures at Balliol and Mansfield Colleges. Still wearing his saffron robe and carrying only a blanket and a Bible, he made quite an impression on some of England's most elite and educated young men. By Sundar's third lecture in Oxford, hundreds of young men had to be turned away because there was not enough space in the hall to accommodate everyone.

In a newspaper interview during this time, a reporter asked Sundar, "So why did you come to England?"

Sundar replied, "Many Indians say that Christianity is not the real religion of England and that it is not practiced here but is merely an Empire plan to change the religions of conquered nations. So I came to see for myself."

"And what have you seen of this?" the reporter asked.

"I have found that you are a very busy people and that you have so much to do there does not seem much time to think about religion. There is a great deal of materialism. But when I get into your homes and know you, then I find that you do really care about religion."

Following the meetings in Oxford, Sundar traveled on to London, where he met privately with the head of the Anglican Church, the Archbishop of Canterbury. The archbishop seemed very impressed with Sundar and offered to sponsor a series of meetings in London. The first of these gatherings consisted of seven hundred clergy of the Church of England who came to hear Sundar speak at the Church House in Westminster.

Then, on March 23, 1920, a large group of missionaries and mission secretaries, representing many missionary organizations in England and Ireland, came together to hear Sundar. He urged those who gathered to learn about the cultures they were going into and to find ways to use as much of the local cultures as possible when presenting and modeling the gospel.

While in London, Sundar was asked to speak at Westminster Chapel. Although this was a prestigious pulpit to be invited to speak from, he told the same simple stories he told when speaking to the people who gathered to hear him in India.

"Once," he began, "I was sitting on a Himalayan hillside, and I looked down on a tree. In the tree was a nest, and on the nest a mother bird was hatching her brood. I knew that a wonderful world was awaiting those chicks, a world of fresh air, green leaves, and sunshine. Soon they would be big enough to leave the nest and fly wherever they chose, but as they pecked their way out of their eggs, they did not know this. The only life they had known was confined to their eggs, surrounded in liquid and dependent upon their mother for warmth. We Christians are like that—the Gospel of Saint Mark tells us that we are not far from the Kingdom of God, just as the chicks in their eggs were not far from the outside world. We do not know what we shall be, nor the things that God has prepared for us. Now, while we are still in the body, our great need is to receive heat from the Holy Spirit."

On Good Friday five thousand people came to hear Sundar speak at the Metropolitan Tabernacle in London. When Sundar rose to speak, the entire congregation stood and greeted him with a traditional Indian greeting. A reporter from the *London Daily Chronicle* was present at the meeting, and the following day an article appeared in that newspaper. Like all reporters, this reporter grappled with what it was that made Sundar so special. In his article the reporter concluded: "How is it that the sadhu has so manifestly captured the religious world within the short space of six weeks?... The secret of this man's power lies in his utter self-abandonment to a high ideal.... It is surely a token of good that we of the West, who are so obsessed with the materialistic spirit of the age, have come in close contact with one who stands for the supremacy of the spiritual."

From England, Sundar traveled on to Scotland and Ireland. At one of his meetings in Scotland, a Swiss pastor was present. When the meeting was over, the Reverend Kiener came to Sundar with tears in his eyes and said, "When I saw you there, standing before me, and heard you speak of your spiritual life, while on the other hand I was surrounded by theological scholars in gowns and hoods, all at once the question came to my mind: What are we aiming at, after all, in studying theology? Why do we learn and study all the hundreds of lesser things, when we do not allow the most important one of all to have its proper place in our lives? What are we doing with all our apparatus of scholarship, and what have we achieved by it all? Men like you can move nations, but what about us?"

Sundar did not answer. He knew that the Reverend Kiener would have to answer for himself the questions he had posed, just as every Christian had to answer them individually.

The following month Sundar spoke in a great missionary conference at London's Albert Hall. Ten thousand people squeezed into the building to hear him speak, while many others were turned away for lack of room. This led to Sundar's receiving over three hundred more invitations to speak in the United Kingdom, but he declined all of them. Sundar felt that his time in England was over and that God had called him to continue on in his journey to the United States.

On May 30, 1920, nearly five months after setting out from India, Sundar arrived in New York harbor. A group called the Pond Lyceum Bureau had offered to arrange a lecture tour of America for him. But soon after disembarking in New York, Sundar learned that the Pond Lyceum Bureau was a business, not a Christian ministry, and that the group intended to make a great deal of money from promoting him. No matter which way he looked at the situation, Sundar could not accept that his religious beliefs were going to be peddled in such a manner. He cancelled the arrangement, leaving him with no itinerary in the United States. He then prayed and asked God to show him what to do next.

Two days later Sundar met a Christian lecturer from Hartford Theological Seminary named Frank Buchman. Professor Buchman was so impressed with Sundar that he offered to arrange a modest tour of the country for him and be his traveling companion along the way.

Sundar spoke at churches in Hartford, Connecticut; Baltimore, Maryland; Boston, Massachusetts; New York City; Philadelphia, Pennsylvania; and Princeton University in Princeton, New Jersey. Sundar was also invited to speak at a conference for Christian students. The conference was being held at Silver Bay on Lake George in New York State, and Sundar made his way there. During the conference he spoke at an outdoor meeting on the shore of the lake. In the early evening, as the sun was beginning to set, Sundar stood with his back to the water and said to the eight hundred assembled students, "America is near the Kingdom, but not of it. Think of it this way. A large tiger was chasing a hunter. But the hunter was not afraid. He knew he was approaching a shelter, and he had in his possession the key to the door of that shelter. But when he reached the door, to his dismay he discovered that the key was no longer in his possession. All that separated the hunter from safety was the thickness of that door. Yet he knew he was doomed. Many Americans are like that hunter. They know where their salvation lies, but they do not make use of it."

Following the student conference at Silver Bay, Sundar traveled on to Chicago and then made his way through Iowa and Kansas before heading to San Francisco.

When Sundar arrived in San Francisco, a reporter asked him what he wanted to achieve while in the United States. Sundar replied, "I do not seek to Christianize America. I come only as a witness of what Christ has done for me. America is already a Christian nation. But although America has many sincere Christians, the majority of the people here have no religion. Here, where it is easy to have religion, where religion is offered on every side, and no one is persecuted for being a Christian, life should be happy and peaceful because of Christianity. But it is not. Instead, there is a hustle and bustle after money and comfort and pleasure, and that all clouds out thoughts of religion. Because it is so easy to have faith in this country, Americans do not appreciate what a comfort there is in religion. At one time the ostrich could fly, but because it did not ever use its wings, it lost its ability to do so. Just so, the people here who do not appreciate the religious faith of their fathers shall lose it."

Sundar set sail from San Francisco on July 20, 1920, and began the long journey home to India. Because no steamers were going directly to India from San Francisco, Sundar was obliged to go to Australia first. On August 7 seven hundred clergy and Christian workers gathered to hear Sundar speak at Saint Andrews Cathedral in Sydney, Australia.

On September 3, Sundar's thirty-first birthday, he was in Adelaide preaching. From there he made his way by train across the Australian continent to Perth in western Australia. In Perth no buildings were large enough to hold all those who wanted to hear Sundar speak, so he held his meetings outdoors in a park. Finally, at the end of September, Sundar boarded a steamer at the port city of Fremantle, bound for Bombay, India.

After a twenty-day voyage across the Indian Ocean, Sundar arrived once again back in his homeland. Hundreds of Indian Christians clamored to hear stories of his trip and his impressions of the West. This is what he told them:

> Many Englishmen of the present-day do not believe in the miracles of our Lord Jesus Christ, and when they asked me questions concerning the miracles, I answered them and added that I saw a miracle wrought amongst them because, in spite of the English people being so materialistic, there were still many spiritual people among them.... There is a good deal of Christianity in America, but that is not enough. Just as a thirsty man cannot quench his thirst even if he is drowned in sea water, because the water is salty, in the same way a spiritually thirsty man cannot quench

his thirst in America because it is saturated with materialism. Our Lord's words, "Come unto me all ye that are heavy laden and I will give you rest," are true as regards the East, but for America our Lord would say, "Come unto me all ye that are heavy gold-laden and I will give you rest."

Still, God has His own witness in the West and all over the world. Sometimes I have heard young Indians say that they do not want missionaries from such places, but that is a mistake. Missionaries from the West who come to India keep the churches at home alive, and if the West did not send its missionaries, very soon their churches would become dead like the Dead Sea. Therefore we should welcome the missionaries for the sake of keeping Christianity alive in the West.

Now that he was back in India, Sundar's mind was once again focused on getting back to Tibet.

Chapter 14

In the Footsteps of Jesus

In May 1921 Sundar set out for Tibet again via northern Kashmir. It was a particularly cold spring, and as he made his way over Rotang Pass, which led to the extreme northern region of Kashmir, heavy snow continued to fall. As a result Sundar found himself clambering along through snowdrifts that were sometimes waist deep. He was bone cold, and as he shivered his way along, he began to notice something he had never seen before on any of his previous trips across the Himalayas. The skin on his legs was beginning to turn a blackish blue color. And then it began to peel off painfully. But Sundar could do nothing about it. Given the extreme weather conditions, he knew that if he stopped even for an hour to rest and take care of his ailing legs, he might well die from exposure, so he kept on moving.

Finally Sundar made it safely to northern Kashmir. There, as he spoke in a number of small villages, his legs had time to heal from the ordeal of crossing Rotang Pass. As he went from village to village, Sundar slowly edged his way closer to the border with Tibet. At the border an enthusiastic young Tibetan Christian joined him, and together he and Sundar crossed into Tibet and began preaching among the villages. As on his previous trip to Tibet, Sundar found the people to be more open and receptive to him and the gospel. And the lamas no longer seemed intent on ordering his execution or meting out some cruel punishment.

Like on the previous trips, getting from village to village in Tibet still proved to be perilous for Sundar. Tibet was rugged, largely barren, and sparsely populated. As a result it was not uncommon for Sundar to travel one hundred miles or more between villages without seeing another dwelling or human being. Although these vast stretches of land were uninhabited by humans, there were plenty of wild animals to watch out for. The two most fearsome of these animals were wolves and wild yaks. Sundar had not had any trouble with either animal on his previous trips to Tibet, but things were about to change.

Sundar had decided to walk on ahead of his traveling companion so that he could be alone to pray and meditate along the way. He had just descended into a broad, barren valley when he heard a strange grunting noise in the distance. Sundar spun around to see what it was, and to his left along the valley he spotted a wild yak racing at full speed toward him. He quickly scanned the surrounding area for someplace to flee to for protection from the charging animal. A stout tree would be the best, but not a tree was in sight. The only place of safety Sundar could see was a large boulder about halfway across the valley. With no time to waste, he gathered up the hem of his robe in one hand and sprinted toward the boulder. As he ran, Sundar looked back over his shoulder and saw that the wild yak was gaining on him. He willed his legs to go faster and faster. At first the boulder did not seem to be getting any closer, but eventually, and with only moments to spare, Sundar reached it. He scrambled up onto the boulder, grazing his shin as he did so, and stood atop it.

Seeing that Sundar had somehow escaped to safety seemed to make the wild yak more angry. Breathing heavily, the beast pawed at the ground with its front hooves, then ran one way and the other around the rock. After half an hour of this, Sundar was beginning to wonder whether the yak would ever tire and let him alone. Another half hour passed, and the yak was still storming around the boulder, as angry as ever, as it waited for Sundar to come down.

Sundar was seriously beginning to consider his options when his traveling companion and a group of traders he had met along the route descended into the valley. When they saw the wild yak and Sundar on top of the boulder, they rushed forward, picking up rocks and hurling them at the yak. At first the rocks only seemed to anger the wild yak further, but the steady barrage slowly weakened the animal's resolve. And when one of the rocks hit the creature above the eye and it began to bleed, the wild yak finally gave up the fight and turned and ran off. Relieved, Sundar climbed down from the boulder and thanked the men for rescuing him.

Just when they thought it was safe to travel on, another, more dangerous menace swept down into the valley and surrounded them. This time it was not a wild animal but thieves. Thieves and bandits were a constant threat when traveling in Tibet, but usually Sundar carried so little with him that they just let him alone. But this time he was standing amidst a group of traders who carried with them all manner of goods and items to gladden a thief's heart.

The thieves surrounded Sundar, his traveling companion, and the traders and, after taking all their possessions, marched them off to a large cave located in the hills on the far side of the valley. Everyone was tense, and Sundar knew that chances were good they would all be killed when they got to the cave.

When they arrived at the cave, the robbers argued among themselves about what to do with their captives. As Sundar prayed for deliverance, a deep feeling that he should preach to the robbers overcame him. Despite the possibility that preaching about the Christian God could enrage the thieves, Sundar began to speak. "You think you have taken everything from us," he said, "but I have something more to give to you."

That certainly got their attention, and Sundar used their momentary interest to tell them about Jesus Christ and His sacrifice and death and the gift of salvation He now offered them as a result. The robbers listened intently to what Sundar said. When Sundar finished speaking, the leader of the bandits beckoned him to come deeper into the cave. Sundar eyed the long sword the man carried at his side and prayed that he was not about to be murdered.

The two men walked many yards deeper into the cave, until they came to a small room that had been carved from the rock. Inside Sundar saw a chilling sight. Many human skeletons lay piled on the sandy floor. The thief spoke in a desperate voice as he pointed at the skeletons. "All these men I have killed for their possessions. Will God forgive me?" he asked.

"Yes," Sundar said. "He offers salvation freely to all sinners, even murderers."

"Then that is what I want," the thief replied. "All of this bloodshed has been a terrible burden for me to bear."

Sundar prayed with the man, and then they walked back to the rest of the group. The headman commanded the other thieves to return all the property they had stolen from the group and asked forgiveness from them for stealing it in the first place. Then he built a fire and made a big pot of tea for them all to share.

It was a wonderful moment for Sundar and his Christian companion, but it was nearly ruined when one of the thieves offered Sundar a cup into which he was about to pour tea. Sundar fought the urge to recoil. He had never seen such a filthy cup. He knew there was no way he could bring himself to drink from it, and he politely asked, "Would you mind washing this cup before I drink from it?" He hoped his request would not insult his "hosts."

The thief closest to him smiled. "I will do that for you," he said.

The man took the cup and lifted it to his mouth. Then he stuck out his particularly long tongue and licked the inside of the cup clean. Then, with a satisfied look on his face, he poured tea into it and handed it back to Sundar.

Sundar sat in stunned silence. He knew that he could not now bring himself to drink the tea. Instead he tipped it out. The robbers seemed surprised and insulted by this turn of events, and as the tension in the cave rose, Sundar's Tibetan traveling companion spoke up. "You must forgive him. It is the custom of Indians before a meal to rinse their hands and the vessels they will eat and drink from."

The robbers began to laugh uproariously. Finally one of them spoke up. "What a foolish thing these Indians do. It is quite useless. If it is necessary to wash your dishes before a meal, you should also wash out the inside of your stomach every day." With that the men went back to laughing.

An hour later Sundar, his traveling companion, and the merchants were back on their way again, everything intact.

Following his return from Tibet, Sundar spent the winter of 1921 on an evangelistic tour of the Punjab plain and the northern provinces. As he walked from village to village, Sundar found himself thinking about his visit to Europe and America. Although he had found the journey very stressful, he felt that he should go back to the West on another missionary visit. When he returned to Simla after his evangelistic tour, Sundar began making plans to visit Switzerland.

Just before he was about to leave for Switzerland, Sundar received a letter from a man named Sir William Willcocks. Sir William explained that he lived in Egypt and was the builder of the Assuan Dam on the Nile River. He had read about Sundar, and what he read encouraged him so much in his faith that he wanted Sundar to visit him. Sir William offered to help Sundar get a visa to enter Palestine and escort him through the land of the Bible.

Sundar was excited by the prospect. Since becoming a Christian, he had always harbored a secret hope of one day visiting the Holy Land. And now here was an invitation from a man who offered to help make his dream a reality.

On January 28, 1922, Sundar set out for Port Said, Egypt, by steamer across the Indian Ocean and the Red Sea and finally through the Suez Canal. Sir William met Sundar at Port Said, and the two men rode by car into Palestine. Everything about Palestine enthralled Sundar. He had read and meditated hundreds of times upon every event recorded in the New Testament, and now he was able to see those places for himself. He spent hours praying at the Mount of Olives and in the Garden of Gethsemane. He passed through Jerusalem and went on to Bethany, Jericho, and the Dead Sea. He bathed in the Jordan River at the spot where, tradition said, John baptized Jesus, and he visited the workshop in Nazareth where Joseph supposedly practiced carpentry. Time after time as he made his way through Palestine, pausing to pray and meditate, Sundar told Sir William, "Christ is always with me wherever I go. He is walking with me at my right hand."

While traveling in Egypt and Palestine, Sundar was asked to preach in the cathedral of Jerusalem and at a large Coptic church in Cairo. While in Egypt, he also visited a church that tradition said marked the place Jesus and his parents had fled to after their flight into Egypt.

When his tour of Egypt and Palestine was over, Sundar was grateful for the privilege of having had the opportunity to walk in the footsteps of Jesus. He knew that no matter what happened to him, he would always treasure the experience.

On February 27, 1922, Sundar arrived in Lausanne, Switzerland, where the following day he began a strenuous speaking schedule. Since the Swiss people spoke one of three languages, French, German, and Italian, Sundar had to speak through an interpreter. When he had visited England, Ireland, Scotland, the United States, and Australia, he had preached in English, the language that those who came to hear him spoke and understood. But now he had to speak in English and wait while his words were translated into the local language of the group he was speaking to.

Sundar's first speaking engagement was in a town called Bienne. Much to his amazement, over three thousand people arrived to hear him preach. A number of the people who could not fit into the overcrowded hall climbed trees so that they could catch a glimpse of Sundar when he left the building.

The meetings in Switzerland continued night after night in various towns and villages. In Tavannes, Switzerland's clock-making capital, all the workers were dismissed at 3:00 PM so that they could hear Sundar speak that evening. In Neuchatel the newspaper estimated that ten thousand people came to hear Sundar speak.

While in Switzerland, Sundar received invitations to speak in Germany. He crossed the border and began a preaching tour of that country. Over the years Sundar had studied Martin Luther and the Protestant Reformation, and he was particularly glad to visit and see firsthand many of the historic sites associated with Luther. The day after a visit to Wittenberg, where Martin Luther had nailed to the church door his ninety-five theses that sparked the Reformation, Sundar wrote to a friend in a letter, "Yesterday I went to Wittenberg, the Cradle of the Reformation. I saw the house in which Martin Luther used to live, and the Church where he used to preach. On the door of the Church he wrote ninety-five articles about the Reformation, and he is buried in the same old Church. This evening I am speaking in the Church."

Sundar also visited Halle, where professor August Franke had started his famous orphanage and where the Moravian mission leader Count Nicolaus Ludwig von Zinzendorf had attended school, as had George Müller, who had also started a famous orphanage in Bristol, England. From Halle, Sundar went to Leipzig, Hamburg, Berlin, and Kiel. Everywhere he went, immense crowds greeted him, eager to hear the simple message he had come to preach.

From Germany Sundar's tour took him to Sweden, where he caused a sensation. In a letter Sundar wrote, "I am speaking in some of the beautiful villages of this country, and people come from seventy miles to the meetings." In fact, special trains were scheduled to carry all the people who wanted to hear Sundar speak to the meetings. Many Swedes said they had never experienced anything quite like the sensation Sundar caused in their country.

Similar numbers of people gathered to hear Sundar preach in Norway before he traveled on to Denmark. While in Copenhagen, Denmark, Sundar was asked to visit the royal palace, where the dowager empress of Russia lived. The empress wanted an audience with Sundar, and when he inquired as to why, he learned that the dowager empress was the daughter of the king of Denmark and the mother of Czar Nicholas II, who had been murdered along with his wife and children four years before, in 1918. The dowager empress wanted to talk to Sundar about the loss she had experienced, and when the two of them had finished conversing, she asked Sundar to pray and bless her.

From Copenhagen, Sundar traveled on to Herning, Denmark, where fifteen thousand people waited to hear him speak. Total silence fell over the crowd as he delivered his message, and many of those in the audience had tears running down their cheeks by the time Sundar had finished preaching.

From Denmark it was on to Holland, where Sundar talked to university students in Utrecht, dignitaries at The Hague, and housewives in Rotterdam. Not surprisingly, Sundar was totally exhausted by the time he had finished his tour of Holland. He would have loved to return to India right then, but he had promised that he would travel to England and speak at a huge gathering of Christians at a place called Keswick, and he would not go back on his promise. As tired as he was, Sundar crossed the English Channel and prepared to face yet another crowd.

Chapter 15

The Perfect Life

Sundar was tired and unwell by the time he arrived in Liverpool, England. But with great effort he kept his promise to speak at the Keswick Convention. However, as soon as he had fulfilled the obligation, he gladly boarded a steamer and headed back to India. The long voyage did him some good, but he was still tired as he made his way back to Sabathu in northern India.

Back home in India, thirty-three-year-old Sundar made a slow recovery, and during the last months of 1922 he undertook a tour of many large cities in India, including Delhi, Benares, and Lahore. While in Lahore he visited his old school, Saint John's Divinity College, and spent a day with one of the missionaries in the city who still remembered him.

How long ago it now all seemed to Sundar when he had fled his home and set out to follow Jesus Christ, not knowing where the journey might take him or even how long his family would continue to spare his life.

While on this trip he visited his father in Rampur. Sundar found him in good spirits, rejoicing in his Christian faith, but his body was now frail and old. In April 1923, six months after he had visited, Sundar received word that his father had died. According to Sher Singh's will, his estate was to be divided between Sundar and his one remaining brother. The estate consisted of a number of acres of land and a large sum of money. Sundar sighed when he learned the details of the will. He had told his father many times that he did not need financial help, yet he knew that his father had wanted him to buy a house to use as a rest stop between his preaching tours.

As he thought about this notion, the idea of having a house to come home to began to appeal to Sundar. He imagined sharing the place with people in need, keeping one room for himself where he could sleep, pray, and write books. And so he decided to accept the money from his father's estate, but he turned the land over to his brother so that the parcel would not be broken up.

It did not take long for Sundar to find just the house he was looking for. It was an old mission house situated in the middle of the poorest area of Sabathu. Sundar knew it was not the type of grand house his father would have wanted him to spend the inheritance on, but he did not care. He felt comfortable in the place and soon invited his friend Dr. Peoples from the leper hospital and his family to move in with him. Dr. Peoples, his wife, and their four children were delighted with the new housing arrangement, which suited Sundar perfectly. Sundar now had a room to come back to whenever he wanted but did not have to worry about who was taking care of the place while he was gone.

Sundar was still tired from his trip to England, so after completing the purchase of the house in Sabathu, he spent the next year writing two books, *Reality and Religion* and *Search After Reality*. These two books were soon translated into over forty languages, and as they were distributed worldwide, requests poured in for Sundar to speak at venues all over the globe. Some of the invitations likened Sundar to Saint Francis of Assisi and Saint Thomas Aquinas. An American writer urged Sundar to come back to the United States for another visit, saying, "You can't make the excuse that India is your own country. Are you forgetting that now you belong to the whole world?" But Sundar refused all of the invitations. He felt that he had already been a witness in the West and that his heart did not belong to the whole world but to the people of the dark country of Tibet.

Sundar tried to go on preaching tours around northern India as much as he could, but his health continued to deteriorate. In 1925 he developed an ulcer in his left eye, and despite the best medical attention, he lost his sight in that eye. However, this did not seem to unduly worry Sundar, who wrote to a friend in Germany:

> As I returned last month from a preaching tour in the villages, my eye became inflamed and caused me great pain.... I am not sorry about this suffering because it is a great privilege to be allowed to suffer in this way, it is a means of blessing for me as it keeps me humble and gives me an opportunity for prayer and intercession. I do not want to be at all sad if I should lose my sight, for God has opened my spiritual eyes which can never become dim. I thank God for this gift and this blessing. I thank you for your prayers and I likewise continue to pray for you.

After losing the sight in his left eye, Sundar found the glare of the sun dazzled him, and he took to wearing dark glasses whenever he was outdoors.

In April 1927 Sundar was determined to return to Tibet. He set out from Rishikesh with a group of Tibetan traders who were returning home via the Niti Pass. They had traveled only forty miles together when Sundar became violently ill. He was suffering from internal hemorrhaging, and the traders carried him in a semiconscious state back to the nearest train station and put him on a train to Sabathu.

When Sundar finally reached Sabathu, he was more dead than alive, but the doctors at the leper hospital nursed him back to health.

Once he was feeling better, Sundar returned to writing, producing two more books and answering the hundreds of letters that flowed in from around the world.

The following year Sundar planned to enter Tibet again, but he waited too long for his Tibetan trader companions to arrive, and by the time they showed up, it was too late in the season to attempt the journey and return safely.

Ten months later, in April 1929, Sundar was determined to make it to Tibet for the summer. He was especially eager to encourage a little band of Christians who lived east of Lake Mansarovar, as well as other Tibetans who were inaccessible to the few Moravian missionaries who worked close to the border.

When he received a letter from a Tibetan man explaining that a group of traders were gathering at Kalka on the banks of the Ganges River in preparation for their trek back into Tibet, Sundar decided to set out to meet them as soon as he could. He had spent much of the winter preparing for such a journey. He had even decided what should be done with the royalties from his books if he did not return from Tibet.

Sundar did not often speak to large crowds now. He relied instead on his pen to do his preaching and on personal meetings with people seeking truth.

But on April 12, 1929, Sundar agreed to speak at the town of Okara. The service was well attended by Christians and a number of Hindus. After the meeting a young Christian sadhu who had patterned himself after Sundar asked for some advice. Sundar told him, "Read your Bible daily with prayer, do not flee from the Cross, and do not become proud when some good people give you any honor. Remember, the colt had the honor of walking on the garments which were spread by men in the way while Christ was entering Jerusalem and people were saying 'Hosanna, blessed is He who cometh in the name of the Lord.' The colt had this honor because Christ was seated on it."

On April 18 Sundar sat down at the desk in his room and penned a letter to a New Zealand missionary he knew and trusted well. The words tumbled out onto the paper. "I am leaving today for Tibet, fully aware of the dangers and difficulties of the journey, but I must do my best to do my duty. But then I set no value on my own life as compared with the joy of finishing my course and fulfilling the commission I received from the Lord Jesus to attest to the gospel of the grace of God (Acts 20:24)."

Sundar stopped for a moment and gazed out the window at the majestic mountains beyond Sabathu. Then he wrote on. "I wanted to come to see you before leaving for Tibet, but I have received a letter from a trader to meet him at once on our way to Tibet. The route will be the same as that about which I told you last year. I hope to be back with one or two Tibetan Christians by the end of June. If anything happens I will send down Thapa to meet you, and if you do not hear anything from me, or about me, then please come to Sabathu in July in order to see to all my things in my house here."

When he had finished writing the letter, Sundar sealed it and picked up his staff and dark glasses. As he had done so many times before, he set off for Tibet without shoes or sandals, clad only in his saffron robe, with a cotton blanket draped over his shoulder.

Sundar's first stop was the leper hospital, where he asked Mr. Watson, the hospital superintendent, to mail the letter he had just written and to take care of any urgent correspondence that came for him while he was away. Then Sundar said goodbye to Mr. Watson and started toward the railway station. Sunnu Lal, one of the Indian preachers at the hospital, waved to Sundar and then joined him as he walked down the hill toward the station. The two men walked quietly together for a mile or so, and then Sunnu Lal turned back toward the hospital. Sundar walked on alone, grateful that he was finally on the way to preach to his beloved Tibetan people once again. This time he was determined to make it all the way there.

On November 18, 1929, the headline in the *Morning Post* newspaper read:

MYSTIC LOST IN TIBET
Christian Preacher Who Visited London

> FEARED VENGEANCE BY LAMAS?
> From Our Own Correspondent, CALCUTTA.
>
> Misgivings are felt among his followers in India regarding the safety of Sadhu Sundar Singh, the Christian mystic and preacher. Not a word has been heard of him since entering Tibet in April on one of his teaching tours.

The Reverend Riddle, the New Zealand missionary Sundar wrote to before setting out for Tibet, along with his friend Dr. Taylor, set off on a twenty-eight-day trip into the Himalayas to see whether they could trace Sundar's footsteps. They hoped to find some news of him, but there was none.

When they returned to Sabathu, they discovered that everyone had some theory as to what had happened to Sundar. Some speculated that he had contracted cholera and his dead body had been thrown into the Ganges River. Others thought that he had probably slipped off the rocky trail and fallen into a ravine, where he perished. Still others guessed that he had made it to Tibet and been martyred there or was set upon by bandits. But no one knew for sure what had happened to Sundar, and since his body was never found, no one ever would know exactly how he had died.

Finally, in 1933, the Indian government declared Sundar Singh officially dead, and his will was executed. According to the will, Sundar left the house and the money from the royalties of his books to be used for training and supporting preachers who worked in Tibet and the Indian states bordering the region. In addition, some of the money was to be used for scholarships for motivated boys from poor Christian families so that they could attend college, and for scholarships for preachers to get further theological training.

As news of Sundar's disappearance and death spread, Christians all over the world mourned his passing. They comforted one another with words from his books and reminded themselves of the things Sadhu Sundar Singh had told them. Sundar had often said, "It is better to burn quickly and melt many souls than to burn slowly and not melt any."

On his last trip to England, as he addressed the Keswick Convention, Sundar had declared, "I feel no fear at the thought of one day dying in Tibet. When that day comes, I shall welcome it with joy. Each year I go back to Tibet, and perhaps next year you will hear that I have lost my life there. Do not then think, 'He is dead.' But say, 'He has entered heaven and eternal life and he is with Christ in the perfect life.'"

After forty years on earth Sundar Singh had indeed entered into the perfect life that he had dreamed of so often as he traversed the Himalayan Mountains.

Bibliography

Andrews, C. F. *Sadhu Sundar Singh: A Personal Memoir*. New York: Harper & Brothers Publishers, 1934.

Comer, Kim, comp. and ed. *Wisdom of the Sadhu: Teachings of Sundar Singh*. Rifton, N.Y.: Bruderhof Foundation, 2003.

Davey, Cyril J. *The Yellow Robe: The Story of Sadhu Sundar Singh*. London: SCM Press, 1950.

Lynch-Watson, Janet. *The Saffron Robe: A Life of Sadhu Sundar Singh*. London: Hodder and Stoughton, 1975.

Parker, Rebecca J. *Sadhu Sundar Singh: Called of God*. London: Fleming H. Revell Company, 1920.

Riddle, T. E. *The Vision and the Call: A Life of Sadhu Sundar Singh*. Delhi: Indian Society for Promoting Christian Knowledge (ISPCK), 1997.

Samuel, M. A. *Sadhu Sundar Singh: The Apostle of the Bleeding Feet*. Word of Christ, 2002.

About the Authors

Janet and Geoff Benge are a husband and wife writing team with more than thirty years of writing experience. Janet is a former elementary school teacher. Geoff holds a degree in history. Originally from New Zealand, the Benges spent ten years serving with Youth With A Mission. They have two daughters, Laura and Shannon, and an adopted son, Lito. They make their home in the Orlando, Florida, area.

Also from Janet and Geoff Benge...

Gladys Aylward: The Adventure of a Lifetime • 978-1-57658-019-6
Nate Saint: On a Wing and a Prayer • 978-1-57658-017-2
Hudson Taylor: Deep in the Heart of China • 978-1-57658-016-5
Amy Carmichael: Rescuer of Precious Gems • 978-1-57658-018-9
Eric Liddell: Something Greater Than Gold • 978-1-57658-137-7
Corrie ten Boom: Keeper of the Angels' Den • 978-1-57658-136-0
William Carey: Obliged to Go • 978-1-57658-147-6
George Müller: Guardian of Bristol's Orphans • 978-1-57658-145-2
Jim Elliot: One Great Purpose • 978-1-57658-146-9
Mary Slessor: Forward into Calabar • 978-1-57658-148-3
David Livingstone: Africa's Trailblazer • 978-1-57658-153-7
Betty Greene: Wings to Serve • 978-1-57658-152-0
Adoniram Judson: Bound for Burma • 978-1-57658-161-2
Cameron Townsend: Good News in Every Language • 978-1-57658-164-3
Jonathan Goforth: An Open Door in China • 978-1-57658-174-2
Lottie Moon: Giving Her All for China • 978-1-57658-188-9
John Williams: Messenger of Peace • 978-1-57658-256-5
William Booth: Soup, Soap, and Salvation • 978-1-57658-258-9
Rowland Bingham: Into Africa's Interior • 978-1-57658-282-4
Ida Scudder: Healing Bodies, Touching Hearts • 978-1-57658-285-5
Wilfred Grenfell: Fisher of Men • 978-1-57658-292-3
Lillian Trasher: The Greatest Wonder in Egypt • 978-1-57658-305-0
Loren Cunningham: Into All the World • 978-1-57658-199-5
Florence Young: Mission Accomplished • 978-1-57658-313-5
Sundar Singh: Footprints Over the Mountains • 978-1-57658-318-0
C. T. Studd: No Retreat • 978-1-57658-288-6
Rachel Saint: A Star in the Jungle • 978-1-57658-337-1
Brother Andrew: God's Secret Agent • 978-1-57658-355-5
Clarence Jones: Mr. Radio • 978-1-57658-343-2
Count Zinzendorf: Firstfruit • 978-1-57658-262-6
John Wesley: The World His Parish • 978-1-57658-382-1
C. S. Lewis: Master Storyteller • 978-1-57658-385-2
David Bussau: Facing the World Head-on • 978-1-57658-415-6
Jacob DeShazer: Forgive Your Enemies • 978-1-57658-475-0

More adventure-filled biographies for ages 10 to 100!

Isobel Kuhn: On the Roof of the World • 978-1-57658-497-2
Elisabeth Elliot: Joyful Surrender • 978-1-57658-513-9
Paul Brand: Helping Hands • 978-1-57658-536-8
D. L. Moody: Bringing Souls to Christ • 978-1-57658-552-8
Dietrich Bonhoeffer: In the Midst of Wickedness • 978-1-57658-713-3
Klaus-Dieter John: Hope in the Land of the Incas • *978-1-57658-826-2*

Available in paperback, e-book, and audiobook formats.
Unit Study Curriculum Guides are available for select biographies.
www.ywampublishing.com